A House Divided?

A House Divided?

Ways Forward for North American Anglicans

ISAAC ARTEN and WILLIAM GLASS, editors

WIPF & STOCK · Eugene, Oregon

A HOUSE DIVIDED?
Ways Forward for North American Anglicans

Copyright © 2015 Wipf and Stock Publishers. All rights reserved. Except for brief quotations in critical publications or reviews, no part of this book may be reproduced in any manner without prior written permission from the publisher. Write: Permissions, Wipf and Stock Publishers, 199 W. 8th Ave., Suite 3, Eugene, OR 97401.

Wipf & Stock
An Imprint of Wipf and Stock Publishers
199 W. 8th Ave., Suite 3
Eugene, OR 97401

www.wipfandstock.com

ISBN 13: 978-1-4982-2447-5

Manufactured in the U.S.A.   07/28/2015

The Scripture quotations contained herein are from the New Revised Standard Version Bible, copyright © 1989, by the Division of Christian Education of the National Council of the Churches of Christ in the U.S.A., and are used by permission. All rights reserved.

Contents

List of Contributors | vii
Preface | ix

1 Introduction: A Year of Fierce Conversations | 1
 —Isaac Arten

2 Homily on 1 Corinthians 1:10–18 | 11
 —David Marshall

3 Life among the Prayer Book–Minded: A Brief History of Recent Anglican/Episcopal Divisions in North America | 15
 —Timothy E. Kimbrough

4 A Gospel Unity | 36
 —John Yates III

5 A Common Heritage and a Common Vocation: Christian Ecumenism and the Anglican Communion | 47
 —John Bauerschmidt

6 A Unity Greater than Doctrine: Ways Forward for Anglicanism in North America | 58
 —Terrell Glenn

7 The Tragedy of Communion | 72
 —Dorsey W. M. McConnell

8 Responses | 90
 Sacramental Relationality | 90
 —Bryan Biba

Gathered at the Foot of the Cross | 94
—Molly McGee Short

A Naïve Hope | 96
—David Wantland

Toward a Shared Narrative | 98
—Michelle Wolfe Howard

9 Homily on Matthew 5:13–20 | 101
—David Marshall

10 Afterword: A Proposal for the Communion | 105
—William Glass

Bibliography | 115

Contributors

Isaac Arten, Master of Divinity 2015, Duke Divinity School

The Right Reverend Doctor John Bauerschmidt, Bishop of the Diocese of Tennessee

Bryan Biba, Master of Divinity 2015, Duke Divinity School

William Glass, Master of Divinity 2014, Duke Divinity School

The Right Reverend Terrell Glenn, Missionary Bishop of the Western Gulf Coast (ACNA)

Michelle Wolfe Howard, Master of Divinity 2014, Duke Divinity School

The Very Reverend Timothy E. Kimbrough, Dean of Christ Church Cathedral, Nashville, Tennessee

The Reverend Doctor David Marshall, Director of the Anglican Episcopal House of Studies at Duke Divinity School

The Right Reverend Doctor Dorsey W. M. McConnell, Bishop of the Diocese of Pittsburgh

Molly McGee Short, Master of Divinity 2014, Duke Divinity School

David Wantland, Master of Divinity 2015, Duke Divinity School

The Most Reverend Justin Welby, Archbishop of Canterbury

The Reverend Doctor John Yates, III, Rector of Holy Trinity Anglican Church (ACNA), Raleigh, North Carolina

Preface

LONG BEFORE I BECAME Archbishop of Canterbury, one of the most important lessons I learned about the Christian life is that it is spiritually unhealthy (and ultimately boring, even depressing) only ever to hang out with those whose views are like my own.

Of course, in the Church as elsewhere we will sometimes want to meet with those with whom we share a particular vision, to plan together, support, and encourage one another. Such forms of gathering, whether informal and ad hoc, or developing into organized movements within the Church, are inevitable and often necessary if we are to harness commitment and energy towards fruitful new projects of service and witness.

But for Christians it can never be enough to meet only with the like-minded. From the earliest days of the Church, we have been taught that our unity in Christ transcends both blood groups and friendship groups.

So although I enjoy being with those of similar outlook to my own, I have increasingly found it to be a vital spiritual discipline as well as a source of great growth and joy to be stretched beyond my comfort zone in the Church. I have gained far more in my own walk with Jesus Christ through being willing to meet with Christians whose traditions and convictions differed from mine—seeking to be as transparent with them as with my closest friends—as from anything else.

Since becoming Archbishop of Canterbury I have had the huge privilege of visiting every province of the Anglican Communion and spending unhurried time in conversation with all its

Preface

Primates. I have been thrilled and humbled by what I have learned of the range of ways, often in the most difficult of circumstances, that Anglican Christians are living out their faith in witness to Christ and in service of a world in need. But it has also become absolutely clear to me that we are now at a time in the life of the Communion when, more than ever before, we all need to grow in the spiritual discipline of learning to handle difference within our unity in Christ. We cannot all travel the world: but we can all choose that journey, because it starts close to home.

Lest that sound like a limp platitude, I shall be specific. The future of the Communion depends on the willingness of Anglicans across our cultural, political, and especially theological divides to spend time together, praying to God, and understanding each other better. Not to paper over differences, but despite them and even through them to set ourselves to discern the presence and work of Christ in each other. That is not something that can happen over cyberspace; indeed I would suggest the global village of instant cross-continental communication undermines genuine fellowship in this respect. I am talking about real-time encounter, which is probably costly, often confusing, but necessarily face-to-face, even eye-to-eye. Our God is incarnational: he came to us in the flesh.

I am painfully conscious that this is not easy. In North American Anglicanism in particular, there are many faithful Christian leaders, on both sides of the current divides, who have been deeply hurt by all that has happened there over recent years. I understand why the prospect of conversation between Episcopalians and other Anglicans can seem foolish or futile. Yet, I pray, the divisions must not become decisive and defining. In light of our Lord's prayer for the unity of all who believe in him, we cannot give up on the task of seeking to live into the reconciliation which he brings. That Jesus voices the prayer in John 17 helpfully acknowledges that the reality is not easy. Yet the choice is not ours to decline. Reconciliation is not an optional extra to the gospel, it *is* the gospel. The world is crying out to be transformed by the gospel, by the self-giving love of Christ. If we could truly demonstrate that gospel in the way we live it together—where self-giving stretches even across the pain of heart-felt differences—then there might be a chance that the world would "get" the gospel we proclaim.

The words of Abraham Lincoln in his first inaugural address are as relevant to the Church today as to the nation in 1861. "We cannot remove our respective sections from each other nor build an impassable wall between them. A husband and wife may be divorced and go out of the presence and beyond the reach of each other, but the different parts of our country cannot do this. They cannot but remain face to face, and intercourse, either amicable or hostile, must continue between them."

So I have been deeply encouraged by what I have learned of the work of the Anglican Episcopal House of Studies at Duke Divinity School, as reflected in this series of amicable and constructive conversations. The contributors to this volume are bold in their willingness to enter difficult, controversial territory, and yet also realistic about the challenges that lie ahead. Pain and perplexity are acknowledged frankly, and there are no naïve proposals for quick-fix solutions. If there is a way forward, it surely arises from the recognition in these pages that Christ is present among those with whom we disagree and from whom we may be formally separated. Such a realization is humbling but hope-giving: it leaves us with no choice but to honor Christ wherever he is recognized and to find ways of connecting across the barriers that have arisen. I commend especially the suggestions made about ways to do this. I pray that all who claim to be Anglicans or Episcopalians across our various churches will reach out to each other face-to-face: at the very least, to talk and pray, and together to find ways to serve the world in Christ's name. This has been aptly named a "roots down, walls down" approach to discipleship.

That such resources should emerge from a collective of bright young students who are eager to change the world—and the Church—beginning with themselves comes as no surprise. That these students will be tomorrow's spiritual leaders . . . now that is news, and cause for rejoicing!

Justin Welby, Archbishop of Canterbury
Feast of St. Cuthbert, bishop and missionary
March 20, 2015

1

Introduction
A Year of Fierce Conversations

—Isaac Arten

The duty of attempting accurately and generously to understand and represent the words and deeds of those from whom we differ has its roots in the doctrine of God's Trinity. The appropriate character of Christian disagreement is a strictly theological topic, and by no means merely a question of church order or Christian ethics. As such, it is, at present, dangerously neglected.[1]

—Nicholas Lash

Nicholas Lash's sobering assessment of the state of Christian practices of disagreement seems nowhere better reflected than in the anathemas and statements of impaired relationship thrown back and forth by members of the Anglican Communion over the past several decades. As various Anglican bodies have attempted to articulate a faithful and compassionate treatment of human

1. Lash, *Theology for Pilgrims*, 46.

sexuality and identify "fit persons"[2] for the ministries of the priesthood and the episcopate, these pressing and visible issues intersect with broader and older matters involving principles of scriptural interpretation, sacramental theology, and ecclesial authority. In the resulting melee, marked by lawsuits, congregational splits, and a general obscuring of the Church's ability to "restore all people to unity with God and each other in Christ,"[3] the ability of any Anglican group to speak "accurately and generously" of any other often seems to be the first casualty.

In the midst of this contention, the Anglican Episcopal House of Studies (AEHS) at Duke Divinity School exists, in Bishop Dorsey McConnell's words, as "a happy anomaly." During the two or three years they spend working toward their degrees, members of AEHS from The Episcopal Church (TEC), the Anglican Church in North America (ACNA), and the Province de l'Eglise Anglicane au Rwanda en USA (PEAR-USA), and other groups worship, study, serve, and share meals together as members of a single organization. These interactions are built into the design of the House and its program of Anglican Spiritual Formation: for example, as AEHS's directors organize students into weekly "listening groups" (small gatherings designed to provide support and accountability and enable continuing vocational discernment), they intentionally combine students affiliated with the various Anglican bodies represented in the House, so that the discussion and discernment that takes place in these groups will include diverse perspectives. The efforts to ensure that Episcopal and other Anglican students encounter and learn from each other while working toward their Master of Divinity degrees form an important part of the public identity of the House as well. Due in part to the House's stated commitment to "maintaining conversation and communion [among the] different Anglican institutional affiliations now represented among its students,"[4] and the expressions of that commitment

2. Episcopal Church, *Book of Common Prayer*, 256.
3. Ibid., 855.
4. Anglican Episcopal House of Studies, "Frequently Asked Questions," http://divinity.duke.edu/initiatives-centers/aehs/what-students-need-know.

in House worship, coursework, and social gatherings, incoming students expect opportunities to share time and space across the boundaries of specific Anglican bodies, and current students appreciate the connections they have made because of them.

Three major factors contribute to the striking collegiality among House members. First, AEHS is located in the broader ecumenical context of Duke Divinity School (DDS), a United Methodist seminary. Since Episcopalians and other Anglicans are themselves guests among the Methodists and Baptists who make up the majority of DDS's student body, no Anglican group is able to claim a dominant position over the others. Since the House was established in 2006, when multiple Anglican groups were already operating in the United States, and its membership always included representatives from a variety of these bodies, AEHS is not historically associated with any one expression exclusively, but with the Anglican identity (in its theology and practice) more broadly conceived. This ability to live, worship, and study as participants in the worldwide Anglican Communion and inheritors of its rich history without limiting the House's identification with Anglicanism to one specific confessional form is furthered by AEHS's leadership. To date, both of the House's Directors—Dr. Jo Bailey Wells (currently chaplain to Archbishop of Canterbury Justin Welby) and Dr. David Marshall (formerly chaplain to Archbishop of Canterbury Rowan Williams)—have been members of the Church of England. As such, the leadership of AEHS has enjoyed a certain distance from the specific commitments and positions that characterize the North American Anglican bodies.

Second, the major divisions between Episcopalians and other Anglicans in the United States predate many House members' identification with Anglicanism. When asked to share how they came to be associated with TEC or ACNA or PEAR-USA, AEHS members frequently describe the way a particular Episcopal or other Anglican congregation welcomed them when they visited while attending college or moving to a new city, and now simply feels like home. Thus their membership was a response to Christian hospitality and liturgy rather than a means of directly protesting

A House Divided?

some ecclesiastical overreach (although a certain number did choose to affiliate with Episcopalians or one of the other Anglican bodies out of theological conviction). While all of the congregations that nurture AEHS students have been shaped in profound ways by the Communion's recent, often traumatic, conflicts, not all of them are currently involved in them at the local level. The existence of a variety of Anglican groups is simply a given in the daily experience of congregations and the AEHS students who belong to them. The given-ness of the separation between various kinds of Anglicans in the United States is unfortunate in at least one respect: it has the potential to blunt or obscure the tragedy of their divisions.

Third, for many AEHS students the effects of the Church's divisions are not yet personal because, as seminarians, only a few have previously occupied positions of pastoral authority or been called upon to articulate definitive doctrinal positions as the representative voice of a congregation. Yet questions of theological commitments, sacramental practice, and ecclesial authority begin to affect seminarians and their families during the ordination process. Sponsoring bishops begin to set expectations and give instructions that may limit interactions across group boundaries, and ministerial internships reveal each group's attitude toward the others at the congregational level. One of the most acute points at which divisions begin to appear is when a House member is ordained a deacon, which may occur while he or she is still taking divinity school courses. Both seminarians and their families face important questions at these points: Should an Episcopal student attend or participate in an ordination service for an Anglican deacon? May an Anglican student receive the Eucharist at the congregation where he or she goes to hear a fellow AEHS student preach? Beneath procedural questions like these, the awareness of ecclesial conflict that comes with the ordination process raises the larger issue of whether Episcopalians and members of other Anglican bodies are able, or permitted, to recognize the universal Church in each other's places and patterns of worship.[5]

Over the course of their training, in official interactions (ordinations, celebrations of the Eucharist, and the like) as well as in less formal settings (House social events, class discussions, conversations over drinks, and so forth) Episcopal and other Anglican students begin to notice that the harmony experienced by House members training for ministry is neither perfect nor guaranteed beyond the cloistered grounds of Duke Divinity School. Additionally, the ordination process and ministerial development during the internships required in DDS's course of study remind AEHS students that the ministries for which they prepare will take place amid, and be informed by, the real theological and ecclesiastical differences that characterize the tumultuous relationship between TEC and other Anglican bodies in the United States. The conflicts that produced the separation between TEC and ACNA, or TEC and PEAR-USA, have unavoidably occurred, and they set the conditions under which members of the different groups encounter each other. As the situation stands, no amount of study or personal friendship can either set the clock back to before those events took place or produce an easy resolution. A clear understanding of the questions and events that produced the Church's divisions remains important, but the opportunity for constructive work lies ahead, in proposing and evaluating possible futures for the Anglican Communion as a whole and in its specifically American expressions.

Recognizing the need to prepare to minister to a Church in conflict, AEHS's founding director, Dr. Jo Bailey Wells, issued a challenge to the House when she visited in March 2013: engage in "fierce conversations" about the common life of the Anglican Communion. In calling for "conversations," Wells stressed the importance of thoughtful, intelligent dialogue in which all views could be heard carefully. In describing these engagements as "fierce," she pressed the group to avoid the inhibiting effect of excessively cautious approaches to disagreement and be willing to let differences

---

5. In his essay in this volume, Dean Timothy Kimbrough raises this as a key question for North American Anglicans to consider.

stand out clearly and be discussed with forthright candor. "Fierce conversations," then, would help House members envision and prepare for ministries in Episcopal and other Anglican congregations that contribute to the Anglican Communion's full, visible reconciliation. Instead of retreating into the peaceful relationship between Episcopal and other Anglican students in the House, and thereby pretending that the divisions of the Church would only matter in the context of future pastoral work (or that they could be avoided altogether in a parish that did not experience pressure to reflect on them), Wells dared AEHS to confront the reality of ecclesial conflict by considering it a live component of the shared life of the House and learning to practice a distinctively Christian way of relating to each other in the midst of that conflict.

"Fierce conversations," as Dr. Wells presented them, involved House members explicitly naming difficult topics; demonstrating their passionate commitments to theological positions on those topics; describing the implications of those commitments for the life of the Church; and working to maintain dialogical, scriptural, liturgical, and pastoral connections with each other in the face of the deep disagreements that would result. The invitation to this kind of relationship made two immediate demands on the members of AEHS. First, it called for the cultivation of a certain boldness and willingness to raise difficult or unpleasant topics. Both the topics at issue in the Episcopal / other Anglican debates and the stakes involved in advocating for each side's commitments gave the discussion the power to change people's relationships for better or worse, infusing the conversational process with serious risk. Second, the prospect of "fierce conversations" and the changed relationships they entailed demanded a firm commitment from House members to maintain contact with each other even after points of disagreement emerged.

This second demand made by the "fierce conversations" process is what made it a distinctively Anglican approach to disagreement. As a recent statement issued by the Convocation of Anglican Bishops in Dialogue (CABD) affirms, reconciliation among Christians is a fundamental reason for the Anglican Communion's existence as a body and a nonnegotiable component of its vocation.⁶ In CABD's statement, participation in this vocation requires Anglicans to "testify that we find ourselves to be brothers and sisters in Christ Jesus, [although] some have claimed otherwise," and to commit at each stage of discussion "to meeting again."⁷ In recent memory, the public face of conflict among Christians, brought on by the legitimate need to discern faithful from unfaithful doctrines and practices, has too often been characterized by groups of Christians demonizing and excluding each other. This, however, represents an easy way out. It is hardly noteworthy in contemporary discourse when the statement "we'll have to agree to disagree" actually means "we plan never to speak to each other again." It is much more difficult to navigate disputes in the Church in a manner that keeps reconciliation in sight as the ultimate (even if finally eschatological) goal and develops habits for encountering those with whom we disagree that do not rush to declare such reconciliation impossible.

As a first step toward learning to disagree in a way that acknowledges the gravity of Christians' theological differences while demonstrating the love that identifies Jesus' disciples to the world (John 13:35), AEHS hosted a series of formal "fierce conversation" events during the 2013–2014 academic year. At each of these events, following the office of Evening Prayer and a meal, during which Episcopal and other Anglican students shared the stories of the journeys that led them into Anglicanism, a guest speaker responded to the question, "As Episcopalians and other Anglicans imagining the future of North American Anglicanism, where do we go from here?" The essays contained in this volume include the text of each speaker's message and reflections by AEHS students on their experience of the "fierce conversations" process.

6. Consultation of Anglican Bishops in Dialogue, "Testimony of Our Journey toward Reconciliation," 3. CABD's report following its fifth meeting, held at Coventry Cathedral in May 2014, was released after the initial round of "fierce conversations" events at AEHS concluded, but its language reflects the goals and reasoning behind our efforts. The editors therefore wish to call attention to CABD's work as an inspiring parallel.

7. Ibid., 3–4.

A House Divided?

The collection is framed by homilies on the subject of unity in the Church delivered by AEHS Director David Marshall at celebrations of the Eucharist on two occasions during the academic year. Dean Timothy E. Kimbrough provides a historical overview of the history of division in TEC in the United States. This essay illuminates several of the fundamental questions of theology and ecclesial order that underlie the contemporary debate over human sexuality and ministry. With this historical study as the foundation for the series, each subsequent speaker considers a potential source of unity for the future of the Anglican Communion, connecting a scriptural, theological, and historical argument with personal reflections on the experience of Church unity and disunity. Dr. John Yates III challenges Christians to read Scripture deeply together, discovering the "gospel unity" that provides the foundation for every form of Christian life and worship. Bishop John Bauerschmidt proposes thinking about Episcopal / other Anglican debates through two lenses: first, the two groups' "shared inheritance" of Anglican history, theology, and pastoral praxis and second, the ecumenical principles contained in the 1888 Chicago-Lambeth Quadrilateral[8] and deployed to delineate space for dialogue between members of the Anglican Communion and other Christian traditions, most notably the Roman Catholic Church, TEC's longest-standing dialogue partner. Bishop Terrell Glenn frames his remarks around the unity of love; not an emotional concept of love that makes people unwilling to confront real and dangerous error in the interest of "being nice," but the kind of love that is ascribed to God and prescribed for God's people in Scripture (with special emphasis on God's moving soliloquy in Hosea 11): an intentional, tender, harsh, patient love that makes demands on everyone involved. Finally, Bishop Dorsey McConnell describes the Church's mystical unity "in the heart of the Father," which transcends human efforts to divide the Church and inspires efforts to reconcile Christians to each other.

The depth and complexity of the issues addressed by AEHS's "fierce conversations" process ensured that a single year of

---

8. Episcopal Church, *Book of Common Prayer*, 876–77.

consideration by a single group of seminarians could not fully resolve them. Yet if the House could not arrive at a complete resolution by its efforts, its members at least hoped to avoid constructing a facile or artificial point of agreement, either by producing the uneasy peace of an armistice or developing a willingness to tolerate the foibles of those they considered misguided. Instead, the result of the House's participation in this project was the discovery that Anglicans are called to be, in Rowan Williams's description, a community of "trustful interrogation,"[9] in which questions that cannot be quickly and decisively answered are worth asking, and that the community's ministers (ordained and lay) are capable of asking them well and debating them charitably. As a result, the example set by Anglican Christians navigating disputes may contribute to their reputation as "a wise and discerning people" (Deut 4:6) who are capable of participating in God's work of blessing the nations.

In preparing this collection of essays recording the yearlong conversational process begun at Duke Divinity School's Anglican Episcopal House of Studies, the editors and contributors hope to illustrate one community's model of "fierce conversations" on divisive topics directed toward the goal of reconciliation and common witness to the truth of the gospel and the reality of God's renewed creation in which that community participates. The process described in this volume cannot simply serve as a template to be reproduced precisely in other places: AEHS is an unusual community and seminarians, because of their evolving role in the Church, participate in dialogue differently than do lay members of congregations, priests, or bishops. Additionally, the results of the conversations held at AEHS are not yet fully visible; the culture of bold engagement that is the intended outcome is still forming and will change as each new class of seminarians is welcomed into it and leaves its mark on it. Finally, although it may seem an obvious point, the contributors to and editors of this volume have not achieved the Christian unity for which we all so deeply hope. The essays contained in this book represent the various points of view

---

9. Williams, "Trinity and Revelation," 207.

A House Divided?

presented at AEHS's "fierce conversations" events, not a single agenda. No one involved in the production of this volume agrees with every word it contains.

While the AEHS conversational process described here may not be a universal or a perfected model for Christian disagreement, we hope it will be found a useful resource for other communities who are addressing disunity to build on. We urge those communities—especially communities in the Anglican Communion—to create local methods of engaging in "fierce conversations" about the future of the Church and engage with media other than printed text as they do so. Conversations taking place in a divinity school have both a logo-centric bias and a built-in time limit, and no matter how moving and challenging we as seminarians find them, they will only reach their full potential for reconciling the Church if the rest of the Church joins in them over longer periods of time. This book offers a few possibilities for future unity and reconciliation; there are many more to be discerned and tested. As this happens, the long arc of Church history might bend toward reconciliation. After all, as Nicholas Lash hopefully points out, "The Church exists to be a place in which the fact and possibility of friendship among those who had been strangers, of homecoming after exile, might be discovered and displayed."[10]

---

10. Lash, *Theology for Pilgrims*, 51.

2

Homily on 1 Corinthians 1:10–18

—David Marshall

Now I appeal to you, brothers and sisters, by the name of our Lord Jesus Christ, that all of you should be in agreement and that there should be no divisions among you, but that you should be united in the same mind and the same purpose. For it has been reported to me by Chloe's people that there are quarrels among you, my brothers and sisters. What I mean is that each of you says, "I belong to Paul," or "I belong to Apollos," or "I belong to Cephas," or "I belong to Christ." Has Christ been divided? Was Paul crucified for you? Or were you baptized in the name of Paul? I thank God that I baptized none of you except Crispus and Gaius, so that no one can say that you were baptized in my name. (I did baptize also the household of Stephanas; beyond that, I do not know whether I baptized anyone else.) For Christ did not send me to baptize but to proclaim the gospel, and not with eloquent wisdom, so that the cross of Christ might not be emptied of its power. For the message about the cross is foolishness to those who are perishing, but to us who are being saved it is the power of God.

1 Cor 1:10–18

A House Divided?

IN A RECENT ADDRESS to the Anglican Episcopal House of Studies, Duke Divinity School Dean Richard Hays observed that this reading from 1 Corinthians is one of the clearest indicators that the Church of the early New Testament period, far from being a perfect model of Christian unity, experienced many divisions, which Paul describes using the word *schismata*: schisms. The partisan spirit bound up with these divisions is vividly conveyed, with people saying, "I belong to Paul," "I belong to Apollos," "I belong to Cephas," or "I belong to Christ." Different Christians see their membership of the body of Christ differently. They emphasize different human loyalties, different traditions and practices, different understandings of Christ, different experiences of the Spirit. It sounds very contemporary. Much of the present debate over the future of the Anglican Communion revolves around identifying theological and ecclesial priorities around which to organize the life of the Church. Given the resonance between the divisions in the Corinthian church and our current experience, what can we learn from Paul's exhortations?

Paul's most striking move in this passage is that he begins with the divisions at Corinth and then, after a few comments about baptism, makes his way to the message of the cross; as the letter progresses this develops into one of the most profound and paradoxical of the New Testament accounts of the death of Jesus. Paul's path from *schismata* to the cross is not entirely clear, but it is significant that he moves quickly from his distress at these divisions to talking about the cross. Even if he does not explain exactly why, Paul seems to be saying that if his readers want to address the scandal of Christian disunity, they must focus on the cross, itself a scandal in another sense (". . . we proclaim Christ crucified, a stumbling block [*skandalon*] to Jews and foolishness to Gentiles," 1 Cor 1:23).

Christians think of the cross primarily as the act of God that brings reconciliation between sinful humanity and God; but the cross is also the act of God that offers us the way to reconciliation within the fractured human family, divided and torn apart by sin. The Church is called to be the first fruits of that reconciled humanity, reconciled to God and to each other. Paul writes elsewhere of how the great barrier of his day, the division between Jew and Gentile, is broken down by God through Christ crucified, so that a new humanity might be created (Eph 2:11–22). And Jesus, speaking of his coming death as a "lifting up," declares: "I, when I am lifted up from the earth, will draw all people to myself" (John 12:32). The image of all people being drawn to the one crucified Lord is vivid and deeply hopeful. If the fall divides us from God and each other, turning us in on ourselves, the cross releases us from that bondage, opening us up to be united to God, and so also united to each other.

At the foot of the cross, we see ourselves and others in a new light. My instinctive view of myself as right, but unfairly treated, and of others as wrong, threatening and unjust, begins to give way. At the foot of the cross I am confronted with the painful revelation of my sinfulness and all that I have done to hurt others and weaken the unity of the body of Christ. And I also have to see all other people, including all those Christians I find most difficult, as those for whom Jesus died, infinitely loved by God. This humbling, challenging, liberating perspective that the cross generates may not yield instant ethical and doctrinal convergence, may not immediately deliver a united Church, but it does create a whole new way of seeing ourselves and each other, centered on Jesus, crucified and risen. Because at the foot of the cross we also celebrate the resurrection of the crucified Jesus, the opening up to us of a new world of possibilities of reconciled and hopeful living beyond what we can imagine.

Confronted by the division and alienation of the human race, Jesus went to the cross. Confronted by the divisions of the Church, Paul proclaimed the cross. As we confront our divisions we will need to understand and discuss many things, and I do not at all mean to imply a glib dismissal of the need for that hard work. But, in the end, the most important thing we can do for the unity of the Church is to meet, as we do in the Eucharist, at the foot of the cross of Jesus and so also in the light and the hope of his resurrection. It is only here that we see ourselves and one another as we should,

A House Divided?

and can begin to become what we are called to be, together, as the body of Christ.

3

Life among the Prayer Book–Minded
A Brief History of Recent Anglican/Episcopal Divisions in North America

—Timothy E. Kimbrough

"RECENT" DIVISIONS: WHERE TO BEGIN?

> Where shall my wondering soul begin?
> How shall I all to heaven aspire?
> . . .
> O how shall I the goodness tell
> Father, which Thou to me hast showed?[1]

It's hard to know exactly where to begin in the telling of this story. We could, I suppose, imagine that "recent" in the context of the Church of England's history might include tensions and divi-

---

1. Wesley, *Manuscript Journal*, 1:109, 111. An excerpt from the so-called "conversion" hymn of Charles Wesley. See his journal entry for May 23, 1738. "At nine, began an hymn upon my conversion, but was persuaded to break off for fear of pride." On the next day his brother John's heart "was strangely warmed," and Charles wrote in his journal, "Towards ten my brother was brought in triumph by a troop of our friends, and declared, 'I believe.' We sang the hymn with great joy and parted with prayer."

sions within the Church in the colonies or at the very least tensions and divisions experienced by the Church in the aftermath of the Revolutionary War. It was no small task to bring a Church together from disparate former colonies, much less to figure out how some continuity might proceed from the Mother Church. At a bare minimum, requirements to pray for the new president of the United States, for some clergy and vestries, seemed to endorse rebellion, call for the renunciation of certain ordination vows, and challenge the time-honored and "biblically sanctioned" divine right of kings. For the sake of integrity some clergy and laity returned to England, some left for Canada, and some simply wondered what God had done.

To begin here, however, would play fast and loose with the definition of a "brief" history. Maybe I should understand "recent" to include the last 150 years of worship according to the Book of Common Prayer (BCP) in the United States, perhaps focusing on the divide, schism or near-schism, created in The Episcopal Church (TEC) by the Civil War in 1862. The complexity of the debate, the action, lack of action, and the ecclesiological implications of a new Prayer Book for the Protestant Episcopal Church in the Confederate States of America, are significant and certainly have bearing on the question of reconciliation of the Church in these latter days.

For example, though the division of the Protestant Episcopal Church of the United States of America may merely have been pragmatic point from the vantage of the Southerner, creating a new "Province" within the boundary of a "new" civil jurisdiction, not a few voices in the North imagined that the time had long since passed to address the sin of slavery. At the end of the war, for good and ill, the charity of the then-Presiding Bishop John Henry Hopkins, Bishop of Vermont, almost single-handedly provided for renewed affection and collegiality of bishops, North and South, without further rancor. In an open letter to bishops of the Southern Church, dated July 12, 1865, he wrote:

> I consider it a duty especially incumbent on me, as the Presiding Bishop, to testify my affectionate attachment

to those amongst my colleagues from whom I have been separated during those years of suffering and calamity; and to assure you personally of the cordial welcome which awaits you at our approaching General Convention.[2]

While the specific issues involved are quite different, Church unity remains a central feature of our current controversies. Still, I suspect that 1865 is not sufficiently recent.

Might "recent" include a review of the tensions and divisions manifest in the formation of the Reformed Episcopal Church (REC) just shy of a decade following the end of the Civil War? Here the ecclesiological dimensions of this split were manifold. Theological debate around baptismal regeneration, a "plain" reading of the Thirty-Nine Articles of Religion, renewal of ecumenical spirit directed towards other Christians from Reformed traditions (including the reception of presbyters ordained in other churches, if their ordinations were regular), and concerns around excessive ritualism drove George David Cummins, Assistant Bishop of Kentucky, to resign his office and transfer "his Episcopal oversight to a new jurisdiction,"[3] the REC.

Even if this division doesn't qualify as "recent" it must be referenced, given the "founding" of a new movement, if not a new church/denomination by a bishop, regularly ordained, and in the Historic Succession. Lest anyone suggest that this be irrelevant,[4] I believe that this chapter in the history of Prayer Book Christianity in the United States of America is important to read. At the very least, it presents the way in which TEC and representatives of REC danced with divisions and reconciliation (and the implied interim recognition of one another's orders). In 1988, the General Convention of TEC, following a little over one hundred years of division between TEC and REC, passed Resolution D022, seeking to

---

2. Cheshire, *Church in the Confederate States*, 203. It's hard to imagine such a spirit prevailing amidst the current controversy.

3. Reformed Episcopal Church, "Brief History," http://rechurch.org/history.html.

4. Guelzo, *Irony of the Reformed Episcopalians*.

explore "dialogue with representatives of the Reformed Episcopal Church."[5] In and of itself the resolution as passed is unremarkable except when compared with the original language of the resolution as presented. Though the perfected resolution named the stated purpose of the dialogue as "looking toward the healing of this particular division," the resolution as presented to the General Convention had used the word "schism," as in "looking toward the healing of this particular *schism*."[6] Neither the BCP nor the *Constitution and Canons* of TEC offer any help finding a distinction between these words, "division" and "schism," yet common parlance suggests diplomacy and grace at work, if not ecclesiological contrast.

RENEWED PRESSURE ALONG HISTORIC FAULT LINES: TWENTIETH-CENTURY QUESTIONS OF THEOLOGY, GENDER, AND SEXUALITY

If neither the tensions and divisions of the 1780s nor those of the 1880s[7] qualify as "recent," perhaps the tensions and divisions in TEC manifest in the 1980s will. Twelve years of preparations for the unveiling of *The Book of Common Prayer 1979* found the visible unity of TEC under attack. Though other Provinces of the Anglican Communion had, in large measure, found ways to keep "traditionalist" and "progressive" forces under the same tent,[8] the practice of the ordination of women to the diaconate and to the priesthood, the debate surrounding Christian holiness and human sexuality, as well as the generally perceived leftward social and political drift of TEC laid bare historic fault lines that would again

---

5. General Convention, *Journal, Detroit, 1988*, 329.

6. Ibid., emphasis added.

7. Also note the creation of the African Orthodox Church in 1921 by African American Episcopalians who believed they had never found their voice and political influence in TEC.

8. Notable exceptions include the Traditional Anglican Communion, the Anglican Orthodox Church, and the Episcopal Missionary Church.

threaten the organic unity of TEC and the understanding of her constituent membership in the Anglican Communion.[9] No clear party alliances along the former "ritualist" / "low churchman" continuum emerged, however. Some Anglo-Catholics supported the ordination of women, for example. Some Low-Church advocates did as well.

The 1977 "Congress of Concerned Churchmen" meeting in St. Louis seemed to be a watershed moment in the gathering of the traditionalist-minded of TEC from whatever walk of life, including from some of the nascent continuing Anglican churches. The manifesto produced by the Congress[10] asserted that churches from which many "delegates" had come had forfeited any authority otherwise conferred by office through their willful break with practices and doctrine (faith and order) of the tradition. This watershed event in the "Continuing Church" movement continues to define notions of legitimate authority in the ecclesiology of many who have now separated themselves from TEC and some from the Anglican Communion altogether.

But if anyone imagined that the Continuing Church movement would produce a united front, nothing could be further from the reality of the ensuing years. Badertscher notes in his thesis *The Measure of a Bishop* that within only four years of the formation of the Anglican Church in North America (soon to become the Anglican Catholic Church in 1978) "there were by one count 23 Continuing Church bishops in nine different denominations," and as of the late 1990s there were dozens.[11]

The ebb of membership in TEC resumed, though not with the pace or vigor that had been hoped for by many in the Continuing Church movement. This was true in part because TEC

---

9. The Anglican Orthodox Church (1963), the American Episcopal Church (1968), and the Anglican Province of Christ the King (1977) had already made moves suggesting the fault lines might suddenly and drastically widen.

10. Anglican Church in America, "Affirmation of St. Louis (1977)," http://www.acahome.org/anglican_documents/anglican_documents_affirmation_of_st_louis.html.

11. Badertscher, "Measure of a Bishop," 3; Prichard, *History of the Episcopal Church*, 265; Traycik, "Continuing Church," 8.

persevered in taking actions offering the traditionalist hope there might yet be a place for him or her in the councils of the church. In 1991, the General Convention passed Resolution A104, "Affirm the Church's Teaching on Sexual Expression, Commission Congregational Dialogue, and Direct Bishops to Prepare a Pastoral Teaching," affirming that "the teaching of The Episcopal Church is that physical sexual expression is appropriate only within the lifelong monogamous 'union of husband and wife in heart, body, and mind' . . . as set forth in the Book of Common Prayer."[12] Lest the resolution embolden the traditionalist, however, it went on to acknowledge "the discontinuity between this teaching and the experience of many members of this body."[13] Three years later in 1994, working to implement canons that were to provide for the ordination and deployment of women in every diocese of TEC, the church continued to reach out to those disaffected by debate on the ordination of women by acknowledging in Resolution C004, "Reaffirm Canon on Equal Access to Ordination Process for Men and Women," that "those who support and those who oppose the ordination of women to the priesthood and episcopate each hold *a recognized theological position in this Church.*"[14] Many who might have contemplated of leaving TEC stayed, and many of the Continuing Church assemblies did not grow as hoped.

As the opening Eucharist of the 2000 General Convention began in Denver, few fully appreciated how the differences in approach to biblical authority and the existing fault lines would soon exacerbate the widening divisions. Prior to the Convention, in 1997, the First Promise Movement had declared the authority of TEC to be "fundamentally impaired" because it no longer upheld the "truth of the gospel." Just a few months after this General Convention, Archbishops Moses Tay (Southeast Asia) and Emmanuel Kolini (Rwanda) would consecrate two priests of TEC, Chuck Murphy and John Rodgers, as missionary bishops and send them to the United States to plant mission churches in the hopes of

---

12. General Convention, *Journal, Phoenix, 1991*, 746.
13. Ibid.
14. General Convention, *Journal, Indianapolis, 1994*, 842, emphasis added.

"rescuing" North America for Anglicanism. This action by Archbishops Tay and Kolini established the Anglican Mission in the Americas (AMiA), a move which came none too soon for some, and to the complete puzzlement of others, not the least those who study ecclesiology.

Some have suggested the whirlwind that surrounded Canon Gene Robinson and the General Convention of 2003 seemed to come out of nowhere. Latter-day historians, however, are able with little effort to trace a direct line through actions of the General Convention from 1979 culminating in 2000 that provided for the possibility of the action that would be taken advancing Robinson to the episcopate. Notably, resolution D039, "Acknowledge Relationships Other than Marriage and the Existence of Disagreement on the Church's Teaching" (2000), lacked in its final form any resolve that might have specifically applied its assertions to same-sex couples. In every other way it allowed for the reader to apply some of the historic "goods" of marriage to other lifelong committed relationships that would by their application designate those relationships as holy.[15] The resolution indicated such relationships were to be characterized by "fidelity, monogamy, mutual affection and respect, careful, honest communication, and the holy love which enables those in such relationships to see in each other the image of God." The resolution would go on to acknowledge that "some, acting in good conscience, who disagree with the traditional teaching of the Church on human sexuality, will act in contradiction to that position."[16] Though other attempts to direct the development of forms for the blessing of same-sex unions would fail at this Convention, few could deny that a significant momentum shift was taking place in favor of some new, refreshed, reformed, or distorted (depending on one's perspective) Church teaching on human sexuality.

During the ensuing triennium the Diocese of New Hampshire would elect Canon Robinson, a longtime priest of the diocese

---

15. General Convention, *Journal, Denver, 2000*, 287.
16. Ibid.

who was divorced, gay, and partnered, as its Bishop Coadjutor.[17] The build-up to the vote in 2003 seemed to embolden constituents of both sides of this divide. If one person spoke of this in terms so glowing that it might serve as a Second-Coming substitute, then another was certain that the apocalypse triggered by the vote would surely bring about the Second Coming. The then-Presiding Bishop, Frank Griswold III, took no direct position on the impending vote of the House of Bishops regarding Robinson's ordination and consecration, but instead articulated several considerations meant to set the conditions for the discussion: the need to respect the action of the Diocese of New Hampshire, the need to recognize in his election the affirmation of a priest who was highly respected, and finally the need to recognize that Robinson was "a fellow member of the body of the Christ, not the symbol of an issue."[18] (In retrospect, Presiding Bishop Griswold's letter helped form a coalition of votes in the House of Bishops and in the House of Deputies that would ultimately secure the successful passage of Resolution C045, "Consent to the Election of the Bishop-Coadjutor-elect of New Hampshire.")

Those opposed to Robinson's consecration as bishop brought their own set of theological and ecclesial concerns to the 2003 General Convention. The minority report of the Committee on Consecration of Bishops on Resolution C045 (2003) urged the withholding of consent to Robinson's ordination and consecration as Bishop Coadjutor of the Diocese of New Hampshire on the grounds that "approval of a bishop elect who is in a same-sex relationship" opposed the teaching of Scripture, the historic teaching of the Church, and the teaching of TEC as expressed by previous General Conventions. The report went on to note that an affirmative vote on C045 would informally approve "the appropriateness of homosexual behavior" without having provided a teaching

---

17. Episcopal News Service, "First Openly Gay Man Elected Bishop," http://archive.episcopalchurch.org/3577_18284_ENG_HTM.htm.

18. Griswold, "Presiding Bishop Writes," http://library.episcopalchurch.org/article/presiding-bishop-writes-bishops-before-general-convention.

to ground the approval.[19] Further, the report acknowledged the strained relationships the action would create in the Anglican Communion and more broadly with other ecumenical bodies. Reactions to Robinson's election occurred outside of the official forum of the General Convention as well, as the Bishop of Pittsburgh, Robert Duncan, and two dozen other deputies appealed to the Archbishop of Canterbury for some kind of "intervention."[20]

Anathemas, mutual and singular, flew back and forth across the Internet, in and out of mailboxes, variously declaring one or another Province "out of communion" or in an impaired relationship with TEC. Archbishop of Canterbury Rowan Williams was quick to establish the Lambeth Commission on Communion (LCC), also known as the Windsor Commission, to study the crisis and to make recommendations to his office. Anglican realignment, however described and experienced, was already underway. Individual parishes, priests, societies, and religious communities explored "alignment" with like-minded provinces and bishops of the Anglican Communion.

ANGLICAN REALIGNMENT AND AN ANGLICAN COVENANT

In March 2005, in response to the *Windsor Report* that was produced by the LCC, the House of Bishops in TEC covenanted not to consecrate any new bishops until the 2006 General Convention and declared a moratorium on authorizing public rites for same-sex blessings through 2006.

Resolution A163 of the 2006 General Convention, "Affirm Pastoral Care for All Members of the Church," provided for the American version of the English "flying bishops" and called the move "Delegated Episcopal Pastoral Oversight," recognizing "the agonizing position of those who do not feel able to receive

---

19. General Convention, *Journal*, Minneapolis, 2003, 222.

20. Episcopal News Service, "Deputies Protest Robinson Confirmation," http://www.episcopalarchives.org/cgi-bin/ENS/ENSpress_release.pl?pr_number=2003-235-A.

A House Divided?

appropriate pastoral care from their own bishops, and [urging] the members of the House of Bishops to seek the highest degree of communion and reconciliation within their own diocese."[21]

Other actions of the 2006 General Convention accentuated the differences between TEC and those who were increasingly estranged from the mainstream of the church and disappointed by the Anglican Communion's general inability or unwillingness to censure the American Church. The election of Katharine Jefferts-Schori as Presiding Bishop of TEC prompted unheeded calls to the Archbishop of Canterbury for "alternative primatial oversight."[22] The Presiding Bishop proposed the creation of an office of Primatial Vicar, though this proposal was not ultimately acted upon. The Convocation for Anglicans in North America (CANA), created by Archbishop Peter Akinola of Nigeria and AMiA, continued to seek the recognition of the Archbishop of Canterbury without success.

In the lead-up to the Lambeth Conference of 2008, the Anglican Consultative Conference (ACC) refused to seat the delegates from TEC and instead asked TEC to account, following the request of the Windsor Commission report, for the "unilateral" action taken in the consecration of Canon Robinson. The then-Presiding Bishop, Frank Griswold, appointed canon theologians, clergy, laity, and biblical scholars to write papers articulating the apologetic of TEC.[23] These papers would be presented and in time gathered

---

21. General Convention, *Journal, Columbus, 2006*, 356.

22. Though the history of the office of Presiding Bishop in TEC, especially recent history, has been one in which the office has accrued various "oversight" responsibilities, the job description presented in Canon I.4a generally shows an office that is administrative and consultative, while urging the Presiding Bishop to "speak God's words to the Church and to the world." The request for alternative primatial oversight seemed confused in light of TEC's historic objection to the use of the word "Archbishop."

23. Some wondered at the time if the Presiding Bishop was the appropriate person/body to make such appointments in answer to the Anglican Consultative Council, given the efforts being made to articulate to the rest of the Anglican Communion how the polity of TEC was less hierarchical than in other parts of the Communion.

together in the 2005 publication *To Set Our Hope on Christ: A Response to the Invitation of the Windsor Report.*[24]

The leadership of TEC had seemed genuinely puzzled at the direct and uncompromising response from leadership in the Global South. Actions taken to remove delegates from TEC from ecumenical dialogue panels of the Anglican Communion and the occasional lack of hospitality shown to the new Presiding Bishop, Katharine Jefferts-Schori, encouraged those seeking realignment with provinces in the Global South, while frustrating others in leadership in TEC who believed that given the set of variables with which they had been presented, TEC had acted and continued to act in the only way that it could (generally articulated by way of canonical conjecture and constitutional constraint).

The Provinces of Rwanda, Kenya, Nigeria, and the Southern Cone were particularly prepared to receive clergy, parishes, and dioceses (San Joaquin, Quincy, Pittsburgh, and Fort Worth) that were seeking to sever ties with TEC.

The Windsor Report had recommended work on an Anglican Covenant. A committee was formed. The 2008 Lambeth Conference managed the brewing controversies, attempting to hold the Communion together, by inviting bishops of TEC to attend with seat, voice, and vote, but without the company of Bishop Robinson. Though some talk of boycotting Lambeth 2008 (to show support for Robinson and dismay at the refusal to invite him) emerged around the water coolers of American dioceses, most bishops attended and participated. The action was not enough, however, to satisfy many of the Global South leadership, some of whom had hoped for a harsher rebuke of the American church and the disenfranchisement of all TEC bishops.

Global South leadership organized the inaugural Global Anglican Future Conference (GAFCON), in essence as a competing or alternative Lambeth event. The "Jerusalem Declaration,"

---

24. Episcopal Church: Office of Communication, *To Set Our Hope on Christ.*

A House Divided?

the signature document produced at the 2008 GAFCON,[25] did not seek specifically to set up alternative judicatories to existing Anglican provinces. It did, however, limit recognition of provincial authority to those "orders and jurisdiction of those Anglicans who uphold orthodox faith and practice."[26] Some bishops attended both conferences. Some Global South bishops stayed away from Lambeth and attended GAFCON as an alternative conference. GAFCON also welcomed some bishops, clergy, and laity from continuing Anglican bodies as yet unrecognized by the Archbishop of Canterbury.

The "final" draft Anglican Covenant, issued by the committee charged by the *Windsor Report*, was put to the Communion in December 2009. The *Windsor Report* had called for three moratoria: on the consecration of partnered gay bishops, on the blessing of same-sex unions, and on the crossing of diocesan boundaries by bishops of one church (province) in order to provide oversight for a marginalized minority within another church (province). The body of the proposed Anglican Covenant text hoped to summarize Anglican identity and polity in a way that provided for unity and diversity within the Communion and for innovation only once considered by conciliar discussion and debate. The four sections of the proposed Anglican Covenant text went through multiple drafts and review before its release, with most of the controversy focused on section four—governing the adoption of a Covenant and its maintenance. Many, no matter the position they held on the Covenant, spoke of the Covenant as being dead on arrival. Few found it necessary to debate the substance of the first three sections (1. Our Inheritance of Faith; 2. The Life We Share with Others: Our Anglican Vocation; 3. Our Unity and Common Life). But section 4, Our Covenanted Life Together, which provided for discipline by the Joint Standing Committee of the Church or

---

25. Global Anglican Future Conference, "Jerusalem Declaration," http://gafcon.org/the-jerusalem-declaration.

26. Ibid.

Province which refused "to defer a controversial action,"[27] proved the occasion for many a blog entry. Milquetoast, said one. A disciplinary clause with no real teeth, said another. It looks too much like a Roman Curia with the Archbishop of Canterbury functioning as the Anglican Pope, said others.

The process of ratification was to have provided for each province of the Communion to weigh in by way of its governing body. As of October 5, 2013, however, only seven of the some thirty-eight provinces of the Communion have ratified without qualification the Covenant (the Church of the Province of Myanmar, the Hong Kong Anglican Church [Episcopal], the Church of the Province of Mexico, the Anglican Church of Papua New Guinea, the Anglican Church of Southern Africa, the Church of the Province of the Southern Cone, and the Church of the Province of the West Indies).[28] Notably absent from the list of those who have ratified the Covenant are the Church of England, The Episcopal Church, the Episcopal Church of Rwanda, the Church of the Province of Uganda, and the Church of Nigeria. The 2012 General Convention of TEC stated in Resolution B005, "Ongoing Commitment to the Anglican Covenant Process," that as "a pastoral response to the Episcopal Church" it should decline to take a position on the Covenant because "there remain a wide variety of opinions and ecclesiological positions in the Church."[29] Nevertheless it felt compelled, in the text of Resolution D008, "Affirm Anglican Communion Participation," to "reaffirm our historic commitment to and constituent membership in the Anglican Communion as

---

27. Anglican Communion: Covenant Design Group, "Anglican Communion Covenant," http://www.anglicancommunion.org/media/100850/ridley_cambridge_covenant_english.pdf, 8. "If a Church refuses to defer a controversial action, the Joint Standing Committee may recommend to any Instrument of Communion relational consequences which specify a provisional limitation of participation in, or suspension from, that Instrument until the completion of the process set out below."

28. Anglicans for Comprehensive Unity, "Status of Covenant Adoption," http://noanglicancovenant.org/background.html#status.

29. General Convention, *Journal, Indianapolis, 2012*, 241–42.

expressed in the Preamble of the Constitution of the Episcopal Church."[30]

Of late, controversy within AMiA over the place of its bishops in the Rwandan House of Bishops led Chuck Murphy and all but two of his fellow bishops to resign from the Rwandan Church and in time to form "The Mission." A meeting in Raleigh, North Carolina, in January 2012 resulted in the formation of the Province de L'Eglise Anglicane au Rwanda en USA (PEAR-USA) to serve clergy and parishes wanting to stay connected with Rwanda as well as those wanting to reconnect with the Anglican Church in North America (ACNA).

With ACNA beginning to approve Common Texts and already living into a distinct set of Constitution and Canons, a family disagreement and division is moving into the next generation of its life. Ways of being Church for some continuing Anglican groups, notably more confessional than those of TEC, (see the emphasis placed on the role of the Thirty-Nine Articles), are becoming codified. The discussion, at least momentarily, is moving away from "What do I need to see in you to recognize 'Church?'" and more toward "Is this what the practice of the Church catholic and reformed looks like?" Apologetics, I think, will become the focus of theological reflection, blog writing, and preaching over the next number of years, as some continuing Anglicans seek recognition by Canterbury and others simply make their peace with some kind of Anglican association, absent membership in the Anglican Communion.

WHY DOES IT MATTER? A PERSONAL REFLECTION

It matters to me tremendously. Ministry from and within TEC was an imperative for me in the late 1970s and early 1980s. This church seemed like the only path available to one who was persuaded that the life of the Church, its missionary zeal, power to persuade, and

---

30. Ibid., 241.

Timothy E. Kimbrough—*Life among the Prayer Book–Minded*

compassionate pursuit of the established kingdom—reformed and catholic—met (like "righteousness" and "truth") in this North American branch of the Anglican Communion. Standing on the shoulders of those who had stood on the shoulders of those who had walked with the apostles was more than simply a romantic notion of pious ecclesiology. It grounded me and seemed to protect me from the vicissitudes of arbitrary debate and compromise. The Historic Episcopate as practiced by TEC opened a window into the Church catholic that constantly amazed me and helped me to begin to recognize "Church" especially in the practices of Baptism, Eucharist, and the office of the bishop.

Without a doubt I numbered among those who would have described the office of bishop as of the *esse* of the Church. Where there is the bishop, there is the Church. The controversies and divisions of the last fifteen years have not led me to despair over the office of the bishop. Surely some have disgraced the office. Surely some have mismanaged their gifts. Surely some have not acted in good faith. Surely some have acted without the full benefit of prayer, discernment, and the gift of the Holy Spirit. But I have not despaired over the office of the bishop. Instead, I am finding my view of the office of bishop evolving. I could never manage some notion that the office was incidental to the life of the Church. That would make me a North American denominationalist or free churchman. But I have begun, in these times of crisis, when ecclesiological norms are challenged at every turn, to look for additional pillars on which the catholic faith and practice of the Church are built. Increasingly, I think of the office of the bishop as of the *plene esse* of the Church (a position held by numerous reformers throughout the ages), only now by diminishment of controversy.

In many ways I cling to the practice of the Eucharist as the sign of catholicity that keeps me in the orbit of the Historic Church. In the light of the practice of the Eucharist, the whole of the New Testament is written. In the light of the practice of the Eucharist, the Church is born at Pentecost. By the light of the practice of the Eucharist, church orders develop and a theology of the sacraments, an articulation of holiness, and end-time expectancy all begin to mature. It is the Eucharist that asks me to be still and gather with other disciples in the name of the Triune God. It is the Eucharist that asks me to hear the Word of God proclaimed. It is the Eucharist that joins my voice with that of saints and angels in the recitation of the Faith once delivered. It is the Eucharist that brings me to my knees for the Confession of Sin and offers God's absolution. And finally, it is the Eucharist that brings me face to face with my Savior that I might "taste and see that the Lord is good" (Ps 34:8). While bishops guard the faithful practice of the Eucharist, the Eucharist itself transcends at least the historical development of the office of the bishop.

It matters: what diocese belongs where; what parish belongs to what diocese; what bishop presides over which jurisdiction. It matters because we must never fail to scrutinize the signs of catholicity that assure us of common mission, common mind, common purpose, and a share in the body of Christ.

If I once tended to be somewhat smug about being a Historic Christian, a Christian for whom the sacramental life, Apostolic Succession, creedal affirmation, and the pursuit of sanctification were important, now I am increasingly clear that there is no place for triumphalism in the Church. We are broken. We have been broken. We will continue to be broken until our Savior comes again. It's not simply that Anglicans might stand up against Episcopalians or other Anglicans. We can also see Methodist standing against Baptist against Copt against Presbyterian. We are broken beyond understanding and yet somehow, in spite of ourselves, I see that God continues to move among us, calling us to hope, to repentance, and to the embrace of redemption. This is, at least in part, derivative of the doctrine of the incarnation—that God would take the broken stuff of humanity and by it incarnate the very presence and mystery and blessing of his Son.

What can we do in the meantime? As dissenting polity structures continue to firm up and seem to force new interpretations of old constitution and canons, it does become harder and harder to find overt ways in which we can work together. In the move from seminary to parish to church council and perhaps, if it may be, to the office of bishop, the clergy of the divided churches will find that the latitude they are provided to act charitably toward the stranger becomes more and more restricted. The ability to interpret and understand the mystery that is Apostolic Succession becomes more and more dependent on particular and sometimes peculiar interpretations of constitution, canon, and rubric. John 17 requires, however, that we must not neglect the effort to see Christ in one another. It is incumbent upon us, for the sake of the gospel, for the sake of the missionary endeavor, for the sake of his body, the sake of justice,[31] it is incumbent on Episcopalians and other Christians, especially other Anglicans, to find the highest degree of communion that we can enjoy.

Some might be inclined to say that absent agreement on orthodoxy we have nothing to share. If that is so, what are we saying about the God who presides over the Church and the lordship of his Son, Jesus Christ? If we weight *our* ability to agree over *God's* prerogative to act and to save, don't we, in part, run the risk of swerving into works righteousness and an extraordinarily low view of sin—a denial of the pervasive effects of the fall? We might likely believe that the Holy Spirit can cleanse and inspire and lead us into all truth. But I believe few among us would be prepared to assert, at any time short of the coming eschaton, that we (or even the Church) might be free from the effects of sin and its power to obscure.

Surely, we have the act of Baptism to share. In the most basic of ecumenical circles and conversations, we've come to understand that impaired communion, defective orders, or even in some cases mutual anathemas do not negate the validity of Baptism. We may baptize together or at least celebrate one another's baptisms together. This is the fundamental building block of Church order on which all others rely. The prerogative of the laity to baptize in circumstances of emergency, the privilege of transferring a baptized individual between our churches without requiring "another

---

31. I use the word "justice" here understanding that it is God's justice we seek: the justice of the kingdom, where the last are first and the first last, where the meek are blessed and the righteous are persecuted.

A House Divided?

baptism," the opportunity to serve as one another's sponsor or godparent for Baptism is clear and unambiguous witness for the ways in which we might work and serve together.

Every effort of prayer and fasting might be done together— the Daily Office, recitation of the Psalter, the Great Litany, the Penitential Order (maybe especially the Penitential Order), and the Supplication ought to be on the list of practices that we might share together. What prevents us from praying together for healing or sharing in the anointing of the sick? What prevents us from burying the dead together? Even at the administration of nuptial blessing, special ecumenically minded canons of TEC would provide for the ordained Anglican not in TEC to serve side by side with the Episcopalian[32] (and if there, then what is the ecclesiological argument for not applying similar discernment in regard to other sacramental sharing?).

On a basic level, unless someone is specifically enjoined against eucharistic sharing by a bishop, I believe that this particular season of life among the Prayer Book–minded still provides for a sharing of our Lord's Body and Blood and that to refrain from the same potentially adds further injury to his Body. During the Commonwealth when some Church of England bishops fled to the Continent seeking refuge, the Caroline Divine John Cosin (1594–1672) found himself estranged from the Puritan-led Church and deprived of his living as a prebendary of Durham Cathedral. He would eventually, after the Restoration in 1660, become Dean of Durham Cathedral, and then bishop. However, from 1644 to 1660 he lived in exile in France. Though his piety was largely formed in the Laudian school, he was noted as having said of the Huguenots while in France, "I never refused to join with the Protestants either here or anywhere else, in all things wherein they join with the Church of England."[33] Likewise John Sharp, the eighteenth-century Archbishop of York who forbade diatribes against Dissenters from the pulpit, "made it known that if he were abroad, he would willingly communicate with the

---

32. Episcopal Church, *2012 Consitution and Canons*, (III.9.6.(c)).
33. Mason, *Church of England and the Episcopacy*, 222.

Protestant churches wherever he should happen to be."[34] Also, Archbishop James Ussher said, ". . . which I do love and honor as true members of the Church Universal, I do profess that with like affection I should receive the Blessed Sacrament at the hands of the Dutch ministers if I were in Holland, as I should do at the hands of the French ministers if I were in Charenton."[35] I don't in any way mean to suggest that quotes such as these resolve questions or complications about whose table practice and authority might be recognized by another. Rather only that for numerous members of the Church of England this question factored in much more than simply the Historic Episcopate, regular ordination, and licensure (essential considerations by contemporary standards). No matter the variation in our Prayer Book editions, we are together the spiritual grandchildren of Thomas Cranmer. He and his successors remind us weekly that no presumption of salvation qualifies the communicant to ford a fenced table ("we are not worthy to gather up the crumbs"[36]). To lead with charity, even from the midst of division, is to risk hospitality, assuming that gospel sanctuary will harbor its own reward.

We can give alms together. We can feed the hungry together. We can visit the imprisoned together. We can work to see that what is obligation for the Christian, that what makes this endeavor of discipleship distinct, becomes possibility for the world.

We surely must be able to study together, sharpening one another's understanding from across the fissure. Doing so accentuates the common heritage and beauty of the Anglican tradition, its worship, its theology, the mystery of life together reformed and Catholic. Studying together in an ecumenical context, situated among Methodists, Presbyterians, Baptists, Lutherans, and Roman Catholics, to name just a few, prefigures the way that seminarians, once ordained, will be situated among the family of churches in the field. It's so artificial, almost numbing, to be educated with the like-minded. No one will serve exclusively with the like-minded.

34. Avis, *Anglicanism and the Christian Church*, 76.
35. Miller, *Constitution and Order of the Christian Ministry*, 171.
36. Episcopal Church, *Book of Common Prayer*, 337.

A House Divided?

Second, sharing the experience of study and the processes leading toward ordination provides the student with the unabashed opportunity to embrace the Prayer Book heritage no matter the church from which he or she comes. The mission-minded may catch some glimpse of the Spirit at work in Church order. The institutionalist may catch the Spirit at work in the ministry of the evangelist. The opportunity is not unique to any one divinity school, but it is unusual and a privilege.

I am someone who, in large measure, takes extraordinary joy in being a Christian, living and believing that Jesus died for my sins and the sins of the world. To stand in the intersection of the sacramental exchange between God and his people enlivens me. It makes me smile. It is my whole reason for being. I can imagine no greater privilege or vocation than to announce Christ's sacrifice and resurrection for the life of the world, to hope in the coming reign of God, and to rest in the assurance that all will be well.

There have been times, especially in the last fifteen years, when this has been hard for me to see, when it seemed that the very foundation on which the Church is built was beginning to erode. But, in fact, I have found that this time of controversy in the Church has deepened my walk with Christ. When everything else seemed to be spinning out of control, the cross of Christ remained at the center of my devotional life and at the center of my heart. I would cling to it when it seemed like the Church was abandoning me. I would hold so tightly to the Tree of Life that my whole week might become consumed with that task. I've cried in my office. I've cried from the pulpit. I've cried in the Rectory. But I understand now more fully than at any other time in my life that the only hope for a seat at the banquet comes not by merit, or right-believing, or just works; the only hope for a seat at the banquet comes by the cross of Christ.

> Lord Jesus Christ, Son of the living God, we pray you to set your passion, cross, and death between your judgment and our souls, now and in the hour of our death. Give mercy and grace to the living; pardon and rest to the dead; to your holy Church peace and concord; and to

us sinners everlasting life and glory; for with the Father and the Holy Spirit you live and reign, one God, now and for ever. *Amen.*[37]

---

37. Ibid., 282.

4

A Gospel Unity

—John Yates III

INTRODUCTION: SHARING PERSONALLY

I BEGIN BY SHARING personally. I am very much what you would call a cradle Episcopalian. I grew up in The Episcopal Church (TEC) and my family has been in TEC for at least the last eleven generations. I was happy to discover this past year that in 1701 my tenth great-grandfather Edward Smithwick (1674–1716) donated a parcel of land in downtown Edenton, North Carolina, for the establishment of St. Paul's Episcopal Church, which is the oldest chartered Episcopal church in our state.

In addition to this long family history, I also happen to be the son of a priest. My father served as a priest in TEC for over thirty years. He was the rector of one of the largest Episcopal churches in the country, The Falls Church, up until 2007 when that congregation voted to leave TEC. He continues to serve as rector of that congregation, which now meets in a prep school auditorium and has been renamed The Falls Church Anglican.

After training at King's College in London and Trinity School for Ministry outside of Pittsburgh, I was ordained a deacon in TEC in June 2003 by Bishop Peter Lee of Virginia. My first position as

John Yates III—A Gospel Unity

a newly minted deacon was as a chaplain at Clare College, Cambridge, England. While in Cambridge I served under license of the Archbishop of Canterbury and during that time was ordained a priest by the Bishop of Ely in the Church of England. Much to my personal relief, the bishop did not require me to swear the oath of loyalty to the monarch, which is a regular part of the service in England and the Commonwealth!

Upon returning to the States in 2007, I worked as a clergy associate at a large Episcopal church in suburban Philadelphia before ultimately choosing to leave TEC in 2010, at which time I relocated to Raleigh and became rector of Holy Trinity Anglican Church. It is difficult to summarize the sequence of thought, prayer, and reflection that go into making a move like I did. On the one hand, it was a very easy decision. I felt that The Episcopal Church I knew and loved had abandoned me and the faith in which I had been raised, forcing me to seek shelter elsewhere.

On the other hand, I knew that to step out of TEC and into the emerging Anglican Church in North America (ACNA) meant to step away from centuries of family tradition and the approval of Canterbury into the uncertainty of a diverse collection of wounded former Episcopalians struggling to create something new. It was not something I did lightly or easily. Although I was not deposed as my father and many of my friends were, as a part of my transition I did receive notice from TEC that in the act of associating myself with ACNA I had chosen to leave the ordained ministry, and as a result I had to walk away from several years' worth of pension savings. These are little things, but they are not light.

I share these few biographical details with you because in the midst of "fierce conversation" it is incredibly important for each one of us to remember that when we engage with others, particularly those with whom we are in disagreement, we are dealing with people who have histories full of joy and full of wounds when it comes to the Church. If you are speaking with a priest in ACNA who is over forty years old, most likely he or she was summarily deposed and removed from his or her office without any kind of recourse. It is very likely he or she lost a church building and personal home along the way. Likewise, on the other side of the aisle so to speak, you may find yourself speaking with a young man who suffered cruelly under the thoughtless pastoral attention of a conservative priest who did not know how to handle his honest struggles with gender identity, refused to listen, and drove him from the community he needed most.

We all have histories. Our histories shape us just as much as, if not more than, our theologies. This is important to acknowledge for two reasons. First, we must treat each other tenderly, because we do not know the joys, the wounds, or the confusion each person carries. But this is important for a second reason as well. We must not allow our histories a greater shaping power over us than the power of the gospel and the Spirit of God.

One of the great adventures of seminary is opening your hands and receiving the work of God in your life as you prepare for a profession that will demand more of you than you can imagine and that will bless you more than you dare to hope. With this in mind, I want to shift now from sharing personally to reflecting biblically.

REFLECTING BIBLICALLY

In order for us to think practically and constructively about the issues that face the broader Anglican Communion and the community you share here at Duke Divinity School, we need to turn to Scripture.

Whether it is the Articles of Religion, the Book of Homilies, Thomas Cranmer's Collects, or our shared Prayer Book tradition, everything in our heritage directs us to Scripture as the first stop on the road to discernment, as the source of our doctrine and as a means of unity. The Collect for Proper 8 captures the essence of this. Here is what Cranmer wrote:

> O Almighty God, who hast built thy Church upon the foundations of the apostles and prophets, Jesus Christ himself being the chief cornerstone: Grant us so to be joined together in unity of spirit by their doctrine, that

> we may be made an holy temple acceptable unto thee; through the same Jesus Christ our Lord, who liveth and reigneth with thee and the Holy Spirit, one God, for ever and ever. Amen.[1]

At the heart of the ongoing conversation we all are involved in is the question of unity. What is the nature of Christian unity? How is it created? How is it maintained? When is it broken? How can it be repaired?

In this essay I would like to take you to Ephesians 4:1–16 because of its focus on the nature of our unity as followers of Christ. We tend to turn to John 17 when it comes to this topic, but I believe that Ephesians is equally if not more helpful in giving us a rudimentary theology of Christian unity.

As an aside, I believe that Paul wrote this letter. Some of you will disagree with that premise. But I think that we can all agree that this letter is among those that have been recognized as authoritative for the Church since the formation of the canon. And it has always been recognized by the Anglican Communion as part of God's authoritative witness to us in Scripture.

> I therefore, the prisoner in the Lord, beg you to lead a life worthy of the calling to which you have been called, with all humility and gentleness, with patience, bearing with one another in love, making every effort to maintain the unity of the Spirit in the bond of peace. There is one body and one Spirit, just as you were called to the one hope of your calling, one Lord, one faith, one baptism, one God and Father of all, who is above all and through all and in all. But each of us was given grace according to the measure of Christ's gift. Therefore it is said,
>
> > "When he ascended on high he made captivity itself a captive;
> > he gave gifts to his people."
>
> (When it says, "He ascended," what does it mean but that he had also descended into the lower parts of the earth? He who descended is the same one who ascended

---

1. Episcopal Church, *Book of Common Prayer*, 178–79.

> far above all the heavens, so that he might fill all things.) The gifts he gave were that some would be apostles, some prophets, some evangelists, some pastors and teachers, to equip the saints for the work of ministry, for building up the body of Christ, until all of us come to the unity of the faith and of the knowledge of the Son of God, to maturity, to the measure of the full stature of Christ. We must no longer be children, tossed to and fro and blown about by every wind of doctrine, by people's trickery, by their craftiness in deceitful scheming. But speaking the truth in love, we must grow up in every way into him who is the head, into Christ, from whom the whole body, joined and knit together by every ligament with which it is equipped, as each part is working properly, promotes the body's growth in building itself up in love. (Eph 4:1–16)

I want to make three observations concerning the nature of Christian unity as Paul describes it and then reflect on the practical implications of what we see here. The first thing to notice in verses 1–6 is that Christian unity is a gift from God. Paul tells us to "keep" or "maintain" it in verse 3. Unity is not something we can construct. It is something we are given and must maintain. The unity of the Church is the unity of the Spirit who has drawn us together through the bond of peace.

That peace is almost certainly not a feeling of peace or tranquility. Paul has already defined peace earlier in Ephesians 2:14–15, where he says of Jesus, "For he is our peace; in his flesh he has made both groups into one and has broken down the dividing wall, that is, the hostility between us. He has abolished the law with its commandments and ordinances, that he might create in himself one new humanity in place of the two, thus making peace." The "bond of peace" (Eph 4:3) that unites us is the blood of the cross, the death of Jesus Christ, by which he reconciled us to God and to one another.

Christian unity, therefore, is not something that we can generate. It is a gift we receive when we turn to faith in Christ and are embedded in his body, the Church. The Spirit of the risen Christ brings this about. It is therefore a fact of Christian existence.

Unity is a gift from God. That is our first observation. The second is that unity is rooted in God's own being. Notice the Trinitarian structure of verses 4–6: "There is one body and one Spirit, just as you were called to the one hope of your calling, one Lord, one faith, one baptism, one God and Father of all, who is above all and through all and in all."

Paul roots our unity in the Holy Spirit in verse 4. We are one people through the Spirit, who bears us up and calls us forward in the hope of new creation and eternal life. Paul then roots our unity in the Lord Jesus in verse 5. Through him we are reconciled to God the Father and share with him as co-heirs of the kingdom. Faith and Baptism, mentioned here, are the internal and external means by which we are united to Christ and thereby to one another in the Church. Finally, Paul roots our unity in God the Father in verse 6. The Father who is sovereign over all things has welcomed us through his Son into the mystery of his own being.

The perfection of this miraculous fellowship that we share is emphasized by the seven-fold repetition of the word "one." There is no doubt in Paul's mind that we have been united with God—Father, Son, and Spirit—and united to one another through God's eternal being.

Christian unity is a gift from God; it is rooted in God's being. Third, Christian unity is a reflection of God to the world. This third point is a logical deduction from the first two and supported by the description of the Church in verses 15–16 as the visible body of Christ.

Here we begin to see the practical significance of Christian unity. If our unity is rooted in God's own being, then our life together is a reflection to the world around us of the integrity of God himself. We—the Church—are like a mirror, reflecting the beauty and glory of God to the world. This is one of the key reasons why Paul urges the Ephesians to maintain their unity. It is incredibly important!

A House Divided?

Now, there is an apparent tension in this passage between the fact of our unity as a gift given by God and Paul's command to pursue it. This tension is captured well by the English Standard Version translation where we are told in verse 4 to "maintain" the unity of the Spirit and then in verse 13 to "attain" the unity of the Spirit. Which is it? In typically Pauline fashion, I think it is both!

The analogy of the mirror is helpful here. I once had the misfortune of dropping and breaking a very large mirror. It was over six feet tall and was mounted in a beautiful hardwood frame. When it fell to the ground the mirror shattered into dozens of pieces, but because of the way it had been mounted the fractured pieces remained nestled in the wooden frame. It was a shattered unity. And in its shattered state it could only reflect a distorted image. Our unity is like this mirror. The Spirit frames the Church, uniting us one to another as a gift for the purpose of reflecting God to the world. When the mirror is whole and spotless, it reflects the beauty of God and the light of his glory into the darkness of our broken world.

This unity, however, is easily shattered by pride, roughness, tribalism, and individualism, with the result that the image of God we reflect to the world is distorted and ugly. How many times have you heard non-Christians say, "I like your Jesus, but I do not like your Church"?

When we are fragmented, we preach a gospel of divine incoherence. That is why Paul urges his friends in Ephesus to maintain the unity established by the Spirit and to work at all times to keep it and repair it whenever it is fractured. This is essential to the Church's vocation as the body of Christ.

There come times, however, when the fragmentation of a church is irreparable and institutional unity becomes a fiction. This happens when there is disagreement over the fundamental tenets of the gospel and basic differences in Trinitarian theology. In these situations, the institutional Church is forced to realign and reorganize. For when there is fundamental and irreconcilable disagreement over the basic gospel message, the institutional Church ceases to exist as a coherent reality.

In this brief look at Ephesians 4, I've said that Christian unity is a gift from God, that Christian unity is rooted in God's being, and that Christian unity is a reflection of God to the world. Unity is something to be fought for and pursued at almost any cost. However, when unity dissolves in the face of fundamental disagreement over the nature and meaning of the gospel, the Church must reorganize. These observations have significant practical application for us in the Anglican Communion and for you here at Duke Divinity School.

If unity is a gift, and if it flows from the being of God himself, then any effort to unite God's people must begin with a humble belief in the gospel of Jesus Christ and the very specific way in which he unites us to God the Father and to one another through the reconciling work of the cross, where he establishes our bond of peace.

The kind of unity Paul describes for the Church is impossible apart from the gospel. To seek unity apart from the gospel is, therefore, spiritually dangerous because it seeks to do the work of Christ for him. When we try to construct by human effort what only Christ by grace can impart, we engage in a form of idolatry.

For these reasons, efforts to unify the Church are, at one and the same time, deeply important and full of human temptation. Christian unity can be a marvelous expression of the grace and goodness of Jesus Christ. Or it can be the futile expression of human idolatry. A patchwork unity of fractured bits of glass built on the back of human endeavor reflects a broken image of God to the world. On the other hand, a humble, Christ-centered unity, gratefully received as a work of the Spirit, reflects the glory of God to a world in need.

REFLECTING PRACTICALLY

We need to begin to think practically about how these observations might shape and influence your common life here at Duke. I'd like to do that by offering four exhortations that I hope will spark fierce and fruitful conversation.

A House Divided?

First, go deep in exploring the meaning of the gospel together.

I am convinced that the most important thing I can say to you when it comes to reflecting on unity and mission is that your discussions must begin with the nature of the gospel itself. What is the good news that you are being commissioned to share as you serve Christ and his Church?

When you finish seminary, you should be able to articulate the meaning of the gospel as you understand it in a coherent manner that can be understood by the average person in ninety seconds or less. That may seem slightly ridiculous, but you will be surprised by how often you will be called on to do this once you are in a parish setting. If you leave Duke unable to do this, then your education will have been a failure and your ministry will be rudderless.

There are a lot of things you all can talk about in the midst of your studies, a lot of very interesting conversations you could have about an endless array of topics. These are important and necessary. It is why you have three years here! But not all topics and conversations are as vital as others. It is important for you to have a firm grasp of Anglican ecclesiology. But it is vital for you to be able to explain why Jesus died on the cross and what he accomplished in doing so.

As you explore the meaning of the gospel, you will need to talk about the nature of what happened on the cross. Our faith converges on the cross and the empty tomb. Likewise our theology converges there as well. By focusing on the cross, you will be forced to talk about the nature of the incarnation, the reality and consequences of sin, the meaning of atonement, the hope of resurrection, suffering, evil, and justice.

Talking about these things will help you to determine what you think the gospel really is. And when you have come to an understanding of the gospel, you will then be able to discern whether you share gospel unity with those around you.

One of the dangerous things about seminary—and to be perfectly frank, a danger that is native to a seminary like Duke, with its strong focus on the academic disciplines—is that you become masters of nuance but novices when it comes to the clear articulation of simple truths. Endeavor to master the essentials. Learn to speak simply and clearly.

As an addendum to this exhortation, let me encourage you to use Scripture as your primary sourcebook when you engage in this deep exploration. Tradition, reason, and experience all play a part; that is for sure. But in our tradition, the conversation begins with Scripture.

Second, be brave in disagreeing.

You are preparing to embark as ambassadors of Christ on a ministry that deals in matters of life and death. When it comes to matters of life and death, it doesn't do anybody any good to sit around trying to be nice. If a man is incorrectly administering CPR on a person and a paramedic arrives on the scene, that paramedic will not say excuse me, or wait for an opportune moment to gently correct; she will push the man aside and take over.

The passion and urgency that emboldens a paramedic in a life-or-death situation should embolden you in your education. You ought to feel strongly about what you are doing here. If you believe that you have been commissioned to shine the light of God into the lives of people around you, then lack of passion about the essential truths of the Christian message indicates a lack of conviction regarding the message, a lack of confidence in your vocation, or a lack of affection for those whom you are shepherding.

Passion is good. I think that is why Jo Bailey Wells described the conversations you need to have as "fierce." What this means is that passions will rise. Faces will turn red. Hearts will beat faster. If they don't, then what are you doing here? As you go about the hard work of discerning the meaning of the gospel, be forthright, bold, and brave in your disagreements. Do not step away from these passions, because they will be the lifeblood of your ministry.

Third, commit yourselves to unity whenever possible.

I will be perilously brief on this. I still have many friends in TEC. These are friends I pray with, grieve with, share with, and break bread with. I consider them full partners in the ministry we have been ordained to, even though we do not share institutional unity.

I believe that institutional unity is important, but secondary to gospel unity—which is shorthand for what we see in Ephesians 4: the given unity we experience when we are bound to one another in and through Christ. Institutional disunity need not impede united gospel ministry in local settings, whether that be between Episcopalians and other Anglicans, or with Baptists and Methodists. This is true in AEHS as well.

Finally, be humble.

Passion and certainty have a way of breeding pride and arrogance. This is one of the occupational hazards that clergy face. It is also an occupational hazard for seminarians. As you study, as you read, as you discuss and fight and grapple with each other, remember who you are. As we say every year on Ash Wednesday, "Remember that you are dust, and to dust you shall return."

You are being trained and prepared for a vocation of humble service. At your ordination you will submit to the authority of the Scriptures and to the authority of your bishop. And you will commit to serving those you are sent to shepherd. These commitments require deep humility and daily dependence on God. Cry out to God for this fruit of the Spirit as you study together.

The best way to do this is to worship together. This is built into your daily life at AEHS for a reason. Daily worship brings you shoulder-to-shoulder into the presence of Almighty God, who alone can lead you into all truth and equip you to serve in the Church.

Here are the four exhortations with which I conclude: Go deep in exploring the meaning of the gospel. Be brave in disagreeing. Commit to unity whenever possible. And, in all these things, clothe yourself with humility.

5

A Common Heritage and a Common Vocation

Christian Ecumenism and the Anglican Communion

—John Bauerschmidt

PRACTICING THE FAITH IN A DIVIDING CHURCH: A PERSONAL INTRODUCTION

I SOMETIMES TELL PEOPLE that I have been working on the subject of division in the Church, and division amongst Anglicans, since the very beginning of my life as a Christian, and that theme has continued. I am from Columbia, South Carolina, and although I was baptized as a child in The Episcopal Church (TEC), I was not raised in the church. I became a believer in Christ and active in the church as a teenager after reading C. S. Lewis's book *Mere Christianity*. I was confirmed in 1976 at the Church of the Good Shepherd in Columbia. This same church went through a division in the congregation shortly thereafter over the ordination of women in TEC that eventually resulted in at least three churches arising from the old body: an Episcopal Church occupying the historic site, a Roman Catholic Church served by a former Episcopal priest re-ordained under the Pastoral Provision of that church, and a Continuing Anglican Church.

I attended Kenyon College and then the General Theological Seminary, where I began my theological education. After ordination in 1984 and my first curacy at All Saints' Church in Worcester, Massachusetts, I returned to graduate school at Oxford University, where I studied with Oliver O'Donovan, at that time Canon of Christ Church and the Regius Professor of Moral and Pastoral Theology at the University, later taking the DPhil degree. I served the Church of England for four years as Priest-Librarian of Pusey House, an Anglican Chaplaincy at the University. I have served as rector of two Episcopal churches in the Dioceses of North Carolina and of Louisiana, and I have served the church in Tennessee for the past seven years as bishop. My spiritual formation owes its largest debt to the Oxford Movement and the Catholic wing of Anglicanism. My brother, Fredrick Christian Bauerschmidt, a Catholic convert from TEC of some thirty years ago, with a PhD from Duke, is a working theologian himself who has written two important books on Thomas Aquinas. The theological project is important to me, and I am also interested in matters ecumenical, with a personal stake in the subject.

So the question is, where might we look for a way forward for two Christian bodies, coupled in their history by division and disagreement, usually mentioned in the same breath as contestants in a yet undecided Anglican future in North America? I hope you will excuse this somewhat bald statement of the question before us, as we try to imagine a shared future for TEC and the Anglican Church in North America (ACNA). The good news, perhaps, is that such a future can be imagined even if the present reality is something less.

SOME ASSUMPTIONS

It might be helpful to begin by laying out some of my assumptions. I am mindful that a rehash of recent history is not really called for here, but that it may be enough to say that ACNA's origins lie in the coming together of bodies (dioceses, parishes, churches, and other organizations) that emerged from TEC at different times and in different ways. The presenting issues of this emergence are variously described, though I think it fair to say that among the "un-biblical" and "un-Anglican" practices identified by ACNA as "accommodated and incorporated" by TEC "in the last decades"[1] are a number of moral issues, especially those which cluster around LGBT persons, which lends a particular color to the division between these churches and to the origin of ACNA itself. I also believe that the words "un-biblical" suggest that, at least in some minds, the moral issues are reflective of more profound differences between these churches about the authority of Holy Scripture and its interpretation.

I am also assuming that these two churches share a great deal of common Anglican history and theology as well as pastoral praxis. These churches will look to the same significant historical periods and to the same movements within the Church for their self-understanding. There may be differences in what is emphasized (two significant identity-forming moments being the nineteenth-century Oxford Movement in England and the twentieth-century East African Revival), but no more within one church than another. In other words, there will be a common spectrum of recognizably Anglican sources in each. These churches will look to common historical figures and common texts, not all of them peculiarly Anglican. Both churches understand themselves as bodies that transcend a beginning in the sixteenth century, and which claim continuity with the great Church of the Creeds and the Councils. This is not to say that this common history is uncontroverted, but that it is of yet not particularly controverted between these two churches. Members of both churches pay homage to the theological legacy of Richard Hooker, for instance, without particular readings of Hooker being identified with either church.

I also assume both complicity and non-complicity existing together as we consider these issues. It would be disingenuous to

---

1. Anglican Church in North America, "Our Genesis," http://www.anglicanchurch.net/media/Our_Genesis_revised_2.8_.13_.pdf, 1.

A House Divided?

ignore the fact that some of us were actors in the story of how we got here, and also that some of us were not. There is an immediacy to these wounds within the body of Christ that, once again, colors this particular question.

It is sometimes observed that newer members of TEC and ACNA were not a part of this story of conflict and division, and that gives them a different perspective from those of us who were. That different perspective will be helpful as we consider the future, yet it is also daunting to think that this new perspective includes viewing each other from an angle that would not have existed before, an angle created by distance and drift. Some of us were leaders in the Church while we were traveling the road that brought us here, at some distance from each other, and we know what the New Testament says about the moral responsibility that leaders take on. Complicity for some of us raises the issue of contrition, confession, and satisfaction as the Church deals with our sins, but it also holds before us the possibility of forgiveness, and the hope of the gospel. That of course is always good news, whatever the circumstances a Christian finds himself or herself in.

THE POSSIBILITY OF UNITY THROUGH TWO LENSES (I): ANGLICAN

As TEC and ACNA consider a future together, I think that it will be helpful to look through two lenses. The first is the lens of Anglicanism and its identity, a lens that we have in common. The strength of this lens is that it is familiar; it brings things into sharp focus and reveals a terrain we know with a mixture of old and new landmarks.

This is very much an Anglican Communion perspective. So here we contemplate a future that is defined by the "Windsor process" outlined in the *Windsor Report*, by which in 2004 the churches of the Anglican Communion were invited to refrain from the consecration of bishops living in same-sex relationships and from cross-border interventions in the affairs of other provinces. It is a perspective that includes the 1998 Lambeth Conference and its teaching on marriage and homosexual practice. It also includes the Anglican Covenant and the "Covenant process" that is ongoing within the Anglican Communion, in which constitutional or other provisions would be adopted in the member churches, creating a means for churches to embrace the old conciliar principle that what affects all is decided by all. This perspective gives prominence to the Instruments of Communion: the Archbishop of Canterbury, the Primates' Meeting, the Anglican Consultative Council, and the Lambeth Conference.

There is of course another perspective here in regard to the Anglican Communion, that of the Global Anglican Future Conference (GAFCON) and the "Jerusalem Declaration": together an additional or perhaps alternative model of binding Anglicans together in a global Communion. Still, the goal is to "reform, heal, and revitalize the Anglican Communion."[2] It is from this perspective that ACNA describes itself as seeking recognition as a province of the Anglican Communion.[3] GAFCON gatherings have included bishops and members of both TEC and ACNA.

Through this lens, the question is one of representation and invitation: of how the member churches of the Anglican Communion relate to each other and how they gather for consultation and counsel. It's a question of membership and franchise. Through this lens, the relationship of TEC and ACNA is part of the disputed and contested relationship between provinces of the same Communion of churches that are deeply divided by the issues of the day and struggling to control a common Anglican future. GAFCON and ACNA may consider the Instruments of Communion as "bruised reeds" (Isa 42:3) that cannot be relied upon when it comes to constructing an orthodox Anglican future, but they are still concerned with an Anglican Communion rather than some other entity. TEC may assert its own inability to adopt the Anglican Covenant, but it

---

2. Global Fellowship of Confessing Anglicans, "GAFCON and the GFCA," http://fca.net/about.

3. Anglican Church in North America, "Our Genesis," http://www.anglicanchurch.net/media/Our_Genesis_revised_2.8_.13_.pdf, 1.

still participates in the Anglican Communion and seeks to shape its future by engagement with the Instruments.

Here we see the limitations of the familiar model in which Anglican churches relate to each other. In an essay published in 2010, Joseph Cassidy imagined a more pluralistic Anglican future, where ACNA might be invited into the Anglican Communion on the condition of its toleration of TEC as part of the same Communion.[4] Such a scenario seems implausible as long as the lens through which we look is the one that peers simply into an Anglican future and seeks to influence and control that future. If the question is the limit of diversity amongst the member churches and the way in which we hold ourselves and each other accountable, then to posit a "tolerant" Anglican future is to answer the question decisively in a way that will not be acceptable to all, in either church.

To view this matter within the terms of Anglican identity and of the future of Anglicanism will get us only so far as we contemplate the way forward for ACNA and TEC. It is a familiar landscape and a worthy subject, but it has the limitation of making the relationship of these two churches a defining feature of that identity and that future. In other words, the relationship or lack thereof becomes itself a contested moment in shaping the future of the Anglican Communion and the identity of Anglicanism. Will it be tolerant and incoherent, or exclusive and confessional? I for one would not despair of avoiding these false dichotomies of an Anglican future through adoption of the Anglican Covenant, honoring autonomy while upholding mutual responsibility and interdependence; I simply point out that the lens of Anglican identity and its future is limited and inherently conflicted in this context as we consider the relationship between the two churches.

---

4. Cassidy, "Radical Anglicanism," in Chapman, ed., *Hope of Things to Come*, 91.

John Bauerschmidt—*A Common Heritage and a Common Vocation*

THE POSSIBILITY OF UNITY THROUGH TWO LENSES (II): ECUMENICAL

So we must try another lens. What does the future look like through the lens of the ecumenical movement, as a not yet realized moment in the quest for full visible unity between divided churches? We must begin by saying that there is at present no ecumenical relationship between ACNA and TEC, no official bilateral dialogue or ecumenical partnership, apart perhaps from some informal conversations and some joint local mission projects. We should also acknowledge that even the appearance of cooperation and dialogue has, in some instances, been viewed with suspicion by members of both churches. So this lens is hypothetical, and not yet really tried, though it is perhaps the case that an event like this one is an example that such an attempt is possible.

In spite of these limitations, something of the spirit and substance of the ecumenical movement is worth capturing as we contemplate the future. Take, for instance, the Chicago-Lambeth Quadrilateral, at the beginning of the modern ecumenical movement that famously articulated four parts of the Christian tradition that would be the basis of the reunion of the churches. The Holy Scriptures, the Apostles' and Nicene Creeds, the Sacraments of Holy Baptism and Holy Communion, and the Historic Episcopate were "inherent parts" of "the substantial deposit of Christian Faith and Order committed by Christ and his Apostles to the Church" (in the words of the 1886 TEC House of Bishops' resolution that first gave official purchase to the Quadrilateral); a deposit that was "incapable of compromise or surrender."[5]

That same resolution spoke of the Savior's prayer in the Gospel of John "that we all may be one": that all the baptized were members of Christ's Holy Catholic Church, that "this Church is ready in the spirit of love and humility to forego all preferences of her own," that this church did not seek to absorb other Communions but to cooperate with them "on the basis of a common Faith and Order, to discountenance schism, to heal the wounds

---

5. Episcopal Church, *Book of Common Prayer*, 877.

of the body of Christ, and to promote the charity which is the chief of Christian graces and the visible manifestation of Christ to the world." The "restoration of the organic unity of the Church" would be a "priceless . . . blessing" to the "divided branches of Christendom."[6]

It is clear that the Quadrilateral is not a statement of the entire Christian faith, but a tool for approaching the question of Christian unity. It is not meant to be a complete statement of "the most important parts" of Christianity, in comparison with which other parts are less important or capable of being dispensed with. It is rather a place to start, the tracing of a trajectory, and an outline of the path ahead. The Quadrilateral set the agenda for seeking unity, and it has been influential not only among Anglicans but also with others. It is part of our common inheritance in TEC and ACNA, and a reasonable place for an ecumenical future to begin.

I assume that ecumenical dialogue is a good thing, inasmuch as it serves the purpose of full visible unity and fulfills the prayer of Our Lord himself (John 17:21). I assume that both churches are Christian bodies, and that the conversation we have is within the family of the Church. I assume that division is a bad thing for followers of Jesus Christ, and that the desire of Christians who find themselves divided ought to be to overcome their state of division. I assume that the ecumenical journey will require conversion of heart, as the Second Vatican Council's Decree on Ecumenism outlined,[7] and generous amounts of charity and humility, as the Quadrilateral says. Forgiveness is not too strong a word when it comes to the reconciliation of Christians to each other.

The ecumenical lens offers another benefit for our two churches. The question of moral discernment and disagreement has become a more and more important topic in ecumenism, as the churches face in common the ethical challenges of modern Western culture. It certainly is at present the topic in the bilateral

6. Ibid., 876-77.

7. Vatican Council II, "Unitatis Redintegratio," http://www.vatican.va/archive/hist_councils/ii_vatican_council/documents/vat-ii_decree_19641121_unitatis-redintegratio_en.html.

dialogue between TEC and the Roman Catholic Church (RCC) in the United States, and I think other ecumenical dialogues are exploring it as well. The question naturally arises as to whether or not differences in moral discernment ought to be church-dividing. This question is, of course, a very acute one for TEC and ACNA since it would seem that the presenting cluster of issues for these two churches is precisely one that involves moral discernment. Yet it is important here to point out that what might divide Christians does not prohibit their conversation, nor does it make impossible the search for Christian unity. The place to begin is at the beginning.

There are advantages in looking through this ecumenical lens. Ecumenism assumes distance while seeking at the same time to overcome it. I think in the present circumstances some distance is a good thing, as long as the distance does not cultivate disregard. The members of our churches have been very much involved in each other's business and continue to be, not least of all in courts of law; presumably these kinds of engagements will decrease over time, though as common inheritors of the Anglican tradition we will continue to inhabit the same space. This is a complicating feature for us, though of course that common inheritance is also a strength.

But looking at each other as Christian churches that are called to unity rather than as competitors for the same ecclesiastical space allows a larger frame to emerge. This lens creates a distance that allows a different perspective, and that perspective is instructive. Distance can build confidence in some cases, and that confidence can then lead to positive engagement. We have issues that must be addressed, but these exist right next to some presumed areas of agreement. The point of the engagement is to overcome distance

A House Divided?

and not to institutionalize it. As Christian churches we need to engage each other, especially if we take the Chicago-Lambeth Quadrilateral seriously; especially if we take Our Lord's prayer seriously.

The ecumenical lens also allows a determined engagement over time. Some are impatient with the ecumenical movement because it does not in all cases yield immediate results. TEC's bilateral dialogue with the RCC has been going on since the late 1960s. This is TEC's oldest ecumenical engagement, and it is easy to question what practical result has been produced, apart from some worthy ecumenical statements. But it may be helpful to ask what our present would look like without this dialogue sustained over almost fifty years. In this case and in others, ecumenical work needs to take a long term view, even when the present prospects are daunting.

The ecumenical lens also allows for difference to be honored without being institutionalized. In ecumenical work you are engaged in a project whose aim is the overcoming of division, but in the meantime difference is honored while the limits of that difference are explored. As Walter Kasper notes, "Dialogue presupposes partners who have, and who are aware of, a strong sense of the identity of their respective churches. Accordingly, ecumenical dialogue has nothing to do with relativism and indifferentism towards the doctrine of the faith. Its goal is not syncretism or unity on the lowest common denominator or peaceful coexistence in division, but full visible communion on faith, sacramental life, apostolic ministry and mission."[8]

Note that this ecumenical lens is not a denominational lens. We are not, I think, talking about arriving at a point where we will be content to look upon each other as different denominations that are seeking dialogue and cooperation, Christian partners who are looking to be good neighbors. We should be seeking reconciliation

---

8. Kasper, *Harvesting the Fruits*, 6.

John Bauerschmidt—*A Common Heritage and a Common Vocation*

within the body of Christ, full visible unity,[9] and full visible communion in faith:[10] the classic goals of the modern ecumenical movement.

I think this is a challenging perspective, to members of both churches. It may not be a challenge that our churches are willing or able to take up at the present, but I think that the challenge will remain, a tie that will tug at us over time. We need to move beyond our un-productive engagement on our common Anglican turf, capitalize on our common heritage, and begin to engage each other as Christian churches with a common ecumenical vocation.

---

9. Faith and Order Commission, "Canberra Statement," http://www.oikoumene.org/en/resources/documents/wcc-commissions/faith-and-order-commission/i-unity-the-church-and-its-mission/the-unity-of-the-church-gift-and-calling-the-canberra-statement, 3.2.

10. Kasper, *Harvesting the Fruits*, 6.

6

A Unity Greater than Doctrine
Ways Forward for Anglicanism in North America

—Terrell Glenn

AS ANGLICANS AND EPISCOPALIANS— WHERE DO WE GO FROM HERE?

Perhaps the best place for me to begin is to tell you a bit about my journey, especially as it relates to this topic. I am currently a missionary bishop of the Diocese of the Western Gulf Coast in the Anglican Church of North America (ACNA). My wife Teresa and I are also planting a church in the city of Houston where we moved just three days before Christmas 2013.

I say that telling some of my story is the best place for me to start because it serves as an example of the mess in which we find ourselves today. I grew up a cradle Episcopalian worshipping at Trinity Cathedral in Columbia, South Carolina. As a schoolboy, I attended St. Andrew's School, an Episcopal boarding school in Middletown, Delaware. While not what one might call devout, my family was faithful in participating in the life of Trinity, the Church, as it would only later become the Cathedral. Perhaps my family's expression of faith could best be described as, "Good churchmanship equaled good citizenship." It was something that good people did.

However, over the summer break after my freshman year of high school, I heard the gospel for the first time. Please know that I am sure that the gospel had been preached many times in my hearing, but I truly heard it with my heart for the first time that summer. What had been distant and irrelevant now was deeply personal and life changing. I came to know that Jesus was God, that he loved and forgave me, and that I could know him relationally. For the remainder of that summer I participated fully in the activities of our youth group, which was led by the newly ordained John Yates Jr. (father of one of this book's contributors).

The fall found me back in Delaware in the routine of religious life at boarding school: mandatory chapel on Sunday and Wednesday and voluntary chapel on Friday evenings. Friday chapel attendance was sparse, to put it mildly. However, a small contingent of us from Columbia who had participated in Trinity's youth group that summer petitioned the chaplain's office to allow us to lead a Friday chapel service. Since the chaplain and headmaster were thrilled over the initiative that we were showing, the evening was turned over to us. We did our best to imitate what had been done for us the previous summer. We offered a few songs (very *Kum-ba-yah*), did a skit, and one of us gave a biblical talk about Nicodemus's encounter with Jesus. We concluded the evening with a prayer in which we asked Jesus to come into any heart that would welcome him. Over twenty students attended. In one evening we had nearly tripled the attendance for Friday chapel. The chaplain, who sat in the back, gave us permission to lead Friday chapel again. This time over forty students came. Same format. Different text. At the end of the evening we offered the idea that people might want to personally accept Jesus as their Savior by repeating the words to a prayer one of us read aloud. Several people did.

There was no third time. The administration pulled the plug, citing the need to get back to the original plan for Friday chapel opportunities. Later I was told that the administration had problems

A House Divided?

with our evangelical approach. It was the first time that I came face to face with exclusion in the Church over theological differences.

During college I was discipled by the Rev. Jim Barnes, a graduate of Reformed Theological Seminary in Jackson, Mississippi, who was serving as an assisting pastor at First Presbyterian Church in Columbia. For three years he grounded me in Reformed theology and taught me how to lead small-group Bible studies. I chewed up the meat and spat out the bones. It was like pre-seminary for me, and it prepared me well for what was next.

After receiving favorable review by the diocesan Commission on Ministry in my senior year of college, I met with Bill Beckham, Bishop of the Diocese of Upper South Carolina, to talk about which seminary I would attend. My first choice was Trinity School for Ministry in Ambridge, Pennsylvania. That idea was rejected outright. I was offered the choice between the General Theological Seminary in New York City, Episcopal Divinity School in Massachusetts, and Virginia Theological Seminary (VTS) in Alexandria, Virginia. I choose the last, as it had become known as the historic bastion of low-church evangelicalism in The Episcopal Church (TEC).

I shall never forget my first class in systematic theology. It was taught by one of the seminary's highly respected and much revered professors. In the first lecture he made the point that he believed in the resurrection of Jesus Christ and saw it as central to the Christian faith. I leaned in from my seat. However, he quickly followed those comments by adding that he also believed that the body of Jesus of Nazareth was rotting in a tomb in Palestine. While I was well aware that seminary would not be some big happy Bible study, I did not dream that I would be presented with this. For a seminary professor to offer the notion that a "spiritual resurrection" accomplished the same thing as the physical resurrection of Jesus was preposterous.

Not that all of my days at VTS were like that. The biblical studies courses under Dick Reid and church history with Bill Stafford were outstanding. The librarian, Jack Goodwin, took me under his wing by introducing me to books that, while not on any syllabus I was ever given, nonetheless found their way to my shelf. However, it became clear to me that evangelicalism was tolerated and evangelicals were marginalized at the historically evangelical TEC seminary. While I contemplated leaving VTS and wondered about why I was even in TEC's ordination process, I was encouraged to stay the more I read and became familiar with Cranmer, Latimer, and Ridley. Furthermore, I found more contemporary fellowship with C. S. Lewis, J. I. Packer, and John Stott. It seemed to me that if there was room for them in Anglicanism, then there was room for me.

After VTS I served a small parish in rural South Carolina in my diaconal year, was an assistant at St. Philip's in Charleston, South Carolina, for six years and rector of St. Andrew's in Mount Pleasant, South Carolina, for nearly a decade. While at St. Andrew's I was a deputy to General Convention in 1994 and 1997. Those two conventions were eye-opening experiences. It was there that I first realized that the real divide in TEC was not over issues such as women's ordination or human sexuality but over the Bible and its interpretation. There was indeed a divide, and it was on a biblical fault line. When the former conscience clause regarding women's ordination was repealed in 1997 through the passage of Resolution A053, it now was a violation of TEC Canons for a diocese to refuse to ordain a woman on theological grounds.[1] This was done without any substantial scholarship on the subject and in blatant contradiction of the tradition and teaching of the Church Catholic. Regardless of one's view of women's ordination, we were now on the slippery slope of mandating behavior that had been neither thoroughly studied theologically nor considered extensively with our ecumenical partners in the Roman Catholic and Orthodox Churches. The 1997 Convention also failed to uphold and require a biblical sexual ethic for the church's clergy and people. For me, it was the writing on the wall. We now were allowing the culture to establish our hermeneutic. It was easy to imagine what would come next.

1. General Convention, *Journal, Philadelpha, 1997*, 112.

A House Divided?

The weeks following the 1997 General Convention saw a series of meetings of concerned clergy. We discussed what we could do to deal with what we perceived to be a crisis of faith and leadership in our denomination. It was in these small informal gatherings that the First Promise Statement was written. On September 9, 1997, a group of TEC clergy endorsed this statement in which, among many other things, we affirmed our first promise of ordination in which we stated that we would "be loyal to the doctrine, discipline, and worship of Christ as this Church has received them."[2] In the First Promise Statement, we declared TEC's Domestic and Foreign Missionary Society and the present structures of the General Convention to have departed from the very promises that we made at ordination, and that the authority of these two entities were therefore fundamentally impaired. We also stated our clear intention to be in communion with that part of the Anglican Communion that accepted and endorsed the principles of the First Promise Statement, and not otherwise.

To say that it did not meet with universal approval would be putting it mildly. Some signers were immediately called into their bishops' offices and told to recant or face serious consequences. At the same time, many others signed on after the fact. By that time, Primates in the wider Anglican Communion were being made aware of the situation in the North American Church. At first incredulous that TEC would reject the clear teaching of the 1998 Lambeth Conference, Global South Primates were soon discussing over thirty TEC diocesan resolutions rejecting the Lambeth Conference's teaching on biblical sexuality. Eventually, two Primates, Archbishops Emmanuel Kolini of Rwanda and Moses Tay of Southeast Asia, requested the clergy of First Promise to nominate two priests to be sent to Singapore. Chuck Murphy and John Rodgers travelled to Singapore, where they were consecrated as missionary bishops of Rwanda to serve in North America. Although criticized for his actions, Archbishop Kolini has often stated that while nearly one million people were murdered in the Rwandan genocide, most of the civilized world knew about it but

---

2. Episcopal Church, *Book of Common Prayer*, 526.

did nothing. When he became aware of the situation in the American Episcopal Church, to him it was nothing less than a spiritual genocide, and he felt that for him to do nothing would be an act of faithlessness on his part. This marked the beginning of the Anglican Mission in America (AMiA).

In 1999, I left St. Andrew's and TEC. A year later my family and I moved to Raleigh, North Carolina, to plant Church of the Apostles as a part of the newly formed AMiA. Although frustrated Episcopalians did join our church, TEC was not our mission field. Most of our members came in fact from other traditions; they yearned for a biblically faithful, liturgical church. We grew quickly. Within four years, nearly 350 people attended Sunday worship services.

After five years at Apostles, I was called to be the rector of All Saints Church, Pawleys Island, South Carolina. It promised to be a fascinating experience, most notably because the parish, having left TEC for AMiA two years before my arrival, was in a lawsuit with the Episcopal Diocese of South Carolina over the property. It is difficult to describe the dynamic this created. South Carolina had been my diocese for most of my ministry. Within months of being at All Saints, I found myself in a county courthouse across the aisle from Bishop Edward Salmon, the man who had only six years earlier been my bishop. He was also a very close friend, so much so that when he would come to our home for Sunday dinner after confirmations, he would feel comfortable enough to go to the stove and eat the lady peas out of the pot before we ever sat down to eat. Now we were in an adversarial posture seeking to resolve a legal question, the answer to which would profoundly affect our lives and those of the people we served. By the time Bishop Salmon retired, the legal issue was still unresolved. Unfortunately, so were the personal issues that crept into our relationship during this process. The distance between us had grown so great that neither of us attempted to make repair.

During my six years as rector at All Saints, I was consecrated a missionary bishop of Rwanda. I eventually left the parish to serve solely as bishop over fifty congregations in AMiA that were located along the Eastern seaboard. With the retirement of Archbishop Kolini in 2010, a level of discomfort arose among key leaders in AMiA because of the leadership style of the new Rwandan Primate, Archbishop Onesphore Rwaje. The Rwandan House of Bishops expressed their desire to have a joint meeting of their house with the AMiA Council of Bishops, the likes of which had never occurred in the ten years of the Mission. They also expressed concern over a lack of financial transparency in gifts from AMiA to the Province. In December of 2011, all but two of the AMiA bishops resigned from the Province of Rwanda. Bishop Thad Barnum and I chose to remain canonically resident in Rwanda and in fellowship with the Rwandan House of Bishops. What followed was a season of enmity, demonization, and slander. Sides were chosen. False accusations were made. In one case, bishops turned on congregations and clergy in ways that were worse than anything that had occurred at the hands of TEC when AMiA was formed in the first place. It was the single most painful experience that I have ever had in ministry. What was most remarkable was that this pain came through relationships with people with whom I had no theological disagreement. But I have to say in all honesty that even in the worst of my disagreements with leadership in TEC, over what I considered to be serious gospel issues, I was never treated as I was during this ordeal.

As I mentioned at the beginning, I wonder if my story is something of a case study for the mess we are in and into which you will be stepping as clergy, if that is how God leads you. In fact, my story is the context for the thesis of my presentation.

There is a unity that is greater than doctrine; it is the unity of love.

> I ask not only on behalf of these, but also on behalf of those who will believe in me through their word, that they may all be one. As you, Father, are in me and I am in you, may they also be in us, so that the world may believe that you have sent me. The glory that you have given me I have given them, so that they may be one, as we are one, I in them and you in me, that they may

become completely one, so that the world may know that you have sent me and have loved them even as you have loved me. (John 17:20-23)

As soon as I say that the unity of love is greater than a unity based on doctrine, I need to qualify it. I am not saying that relationship trumps truth, because truth and trust are the foundation of any healthy relationship. Without trust, I will reveal nothing to you about me that you cannot observe on your own. And what I reveal must be true, or else you are getting to know someone who is not real.

Nor am I equating mere relating or its tools, such as dialogue, with love. By love I do not mean sentimentality or even unconditional acceptance—the family dog can give that. I am referring to the love of God in Christ, the sacrificial, indefatigable, guileless, obedient love demonstrated by Jesus on the cross.

By stating that there is a unity that is greater than doctrine, I do not intend to demean doctrine or the right teaching of the Church in any way. Biblically based doctrine is the body of teaching that the Church possesses by which we understand God as he has revealed himself to us so that we can know him, and by knowing him have eternal life (John 17:3).

And I am aware that I border on a circular logic inasmuch as our understanding of God's love comes from the study of Scripture and the doctrine of God that the Church has formed from it.

So, enough about what I don't mean. What I intend here is to assert that any unity in the Church that has been created only by a shared understanding of the nature of God, the Atonement, the Church, Christian morality, and the like, and that is not held and offered in love, is to be accounted as nothing. Fortunately, I did not just make that up. It is clearly what the Apostle Paul was communicating:

> If I speak in the tongues of men and of angels, but have not love, I am a noisy gong or a clanging cymbal. And if I have prophetic powers, and understand all mysteries and all knowledge, and if I have all faith, so as to remove mountains, but have not love, I am nothing. If I give away

A House Divided?

all I have, and if I deliver up my body to be burned, but have not love, I gain nothing. (1 Cor 13:1–3)

Have you ever considered how much room for doctrinal interpretation Jesus left us regarding the two primary sacraments of the Church? Take Baptism. While Baptism has always been regarded as the entrance rite for the Church, current doctrine and practices roam between seeing it as necessary for salvation to seeing it as optional and for those who just want the experience. In some churches it is offered only to those making their own profession of faith and in others it is available to those who have faith professed for them. As for the amount of water necessary, one can be sprinkled, poured upon, dipped, or plunged, all depending upon the tradition and its accompanying doctrine. Several years ago a clergy group meeting at the parish I served as rector asked the theologian Dr. J. I. Packer to differentiate between baby dedications and believer's Baptism and the Baptism of the infant children of believers. Citing the dedication tradition, Packer responded, "Well, I guess that is a dry Baptism, and their believer's Baptism is a wet confirmation."

It gets no clearer with Holy Communion. Is it a mere memorial? Transubstantiation? True presence? Real presence? Lest we forget, Cranmer, Latimer, and Ridley took attempting to clarify this so seriously as to be burned at the stake over the doctrine of the Church regarding it.

However, for all of the seeming ambiguity here in two sacraments of such importance to the life of the Church, we do well to consider Jesus' robust and thorough teaching regarding love. We are to love God, one another, and our neighbor as ourselves. Moreover, we are to love even our enemies. There is no ambiguity here. Jesus never intended there to be. He told us, "Greater love has no one than this, that someone lay his life down for his friends" (John 15:13). And he demonstrated this by stretching out his arms of love on the hard wood of the cross and offering himself as a sacrifice for sin to make atonement for us all.

There is a unity that is greater than doctrine; it is the unity of love.

To get a picture of this love and where we go from here, perhaps we could look quickly at the eleventh chapter of Hosea, which is a tremendous description of God's love for us: "When Israel was a child I loved him, and out of Egypt I called my son. The more they were called, the more they went away; they kept sacrificing to the Baals and burning offerings to idols" (Hos 11:1–2).

First of all, we see here love's *choice*. Perhaps this is the most important of all of the aspects of God's love in this season in which we find ourselves. God called his people. He chose them to love. The unity that comes from God's love will never be an accident. It always involves choice. It always requires intentionality.

Paul wrote to the Church at Ephesus:

> Blessed be the God and Father of our Lord Jesus Christ, who has blessed us in Christ with every spiritual blessing in the heavenly places, even as he chose us in him before the foundation of the world, that we should be holy and blameless before him. In love he predestined us for adoption as sons through Jesus Christ, according to the purpose of his will, to the praise of his glorious grace, with which he has blessed us in the Beloved. (Eph 1:3–6)

There is nothing accidental there about love's choice. Jesus is so clear about this with his disciples, to whom he says, "You did not choose me, but I chose you" (John 15:16a). Pastor Steve Brown is fond of saying that you cannot love until you have been loved. And you can only love to the degree that you have been loved. The beloved disciple would write, "We love because he first loved us" (1 John 4:19).

As Jesus' disciples today we are to imitate him, walking "in love as Christ first loved us" (Eph 5:2a). This means that our love must be determined and decisive. Years ago I was having lunch with an African American Assemblies of God pastor with whom I would meet every other week. I remarked to him that my church was filled with rich white people and that I wanted him to help me find a way to integrate our worship services. He looked at me and shook his head. "Won't come through programs," he said. "The only authentic way for there to be color around the Lord's table is for there to be color around your supper table." He was describing the deeply personal choice to love.

So, who is at our supper table? Whom have we chosen to love?

This leads us to Hosea 11:3–4: "Yet it was I who taught Ephraim to walk; I took them up by their arms, but they did not know that I healed them. I led them with cords of kindness, with the bands of love, and I became to them as one who eases the yoke on their jaws, and I bent down to them and fed them."

Next, there is love's *tenderness*. This love has a gentleness, a care. It lets the needs of others make a claim on us. On our time. On our energy. On our resources. It is here, I believe, that we have suffered our greatest breakdown, especially among the leaders in the Episcopal / other Anglican divides. We have demonized one another. We have sought to gain a following by proclaiming what and whom we are against. It is the strategy of anti-vision. And trust me, you can raise a lot of money by gathering people with the common denominator of what and whom we oppose. We so quickly forget what Jesus has taught us through his word and also by his actions: "But I say to you who hear, love your enemies, do good to those who hate you. Bless those who curse you. Pray for those who abuse you" (Luke 6:27–28).

Earlier I mentioned the strain in my relationship with Bishop Salmon during the legal process over the All Saints property dispute. Several years later, when I was enduring the difficulties of the AMiA meltdown, I was prayerfully noting to God some of the horrible things that others had done to me. In particular, I remember expressing to God the pain of being demonized by others. While I did not hear the audible voice of God, I distinctly recall a question bubbling up in my soul. As I considered what had been done to me, the Lord challenged me with the question of whether I had actually done the same to others. Bishop Salmon quickly came to mind. He who had been a friend and mentor was reduced in my mind, heart, and speech to others to a place of derision and disdain. I had demonized him. Later that same day I called him. He graciously took my call and listened to my admission of guilt and my desire for his forgiveness. He gave it quickly.

There is a tenderness to God's love that must be found in us. In much of the heated debate over our differences, our reflex is often either to strike back or dismiss others to oblivion with some modern version of the Aramaic term *raca* (Matt 5:22). But love's tenderness requires us to care for others with a deep concern for their welfare. It means willing the best for others and being willing to be used by God in order to get the best for them.

Hosea shows the other side of the same coin in verses 5–7:

> They shall not return to the land of Egypt, but Assyria shall be their king, because they have refused to return to me. The sword shall rage against their cities, consume the bars of their gates, and devour them because of their own counsels. My people are bent on turning away from me, and though they call out to the Most High, he shall not raise them up at all. (Hos 11:5–7)

Here we have a glimpse of love's *harshness*. The writer of the letter to the Hebrews reminds us that it is a fearful thing to fall into the hands of the living God (Heb 10:31). This is because he is God, and we are not. Just as Isaiah quaked before the throne of God in his vision of the Holy Place and the One upon the throne, we must always remember that there is a part of love that will always challenge us, threaten us, and serve as a rebuke to our rebellious hearts. As a result, we will experience love as having a certain harshness because it is abrasive to our willfulness. But it is still love.

There are two extremely important things to hold in balance as we find ourselves disagreeing with one another. First, are we willing to put before God the possibility that we are wrong? And have we asked God to show us if we are, in fact, wrong? Paul reminds the Philippian church of God's readiness to correct us in our humility: "Let those of us who are mature think this way, and if in anything you think otherwise, God will reveal that also to you" (Phil 3:15). The second stems from the first. We must not shrink back from telling the truth. As we humbly submit our opinions and convictions to God for correction, we cannot withhold truth from others just to be polite. We cannot go along to get along. That is not love. Surely this is much of what Bishop FitzSimons Allison

A House Divided?

is getting at in his book *The Cruelty of Heresy*.[3] Heresy is evil not merely because it is untrue. It has pastoral implications as well. To teach or lead others to believe that a certain thing is true and good when in reality it is not is actually cruelty. If I truly believe that a certain behavior will lead to destruction or imperil one's soul and I say nothing to the person following that path, how am I loving that person? It is here that love's tension can be at its greatest. Yet we must remember that in Jesus' teaching about restoration of relationships in Matthew 18:15–18, the final recourse is to treat the offender as a tax collector or sinner, and the gospel accounts repeatedly demonstrate the welcome Jesus extended to them.

Toward the end of Hosea 11 we read of two final aspects of God's love:

> How can I give you up, O Ephraim? How can I hand you over, O Israel? How can I make you like Admah? How can I treat you like Zeboiim? My heart recoils within me; my compassion grows warm and tender. I will not execute my burning anger; I will not again destroy Ephraim; for I am God and not a man, the Holy one in your midst, and I will not come in wrath. They shall go after the Lord; he will roar like a lion; when he roars, his children shall come trembling from the west; they shall come trembling like birds from Egypt, and like doves from the land of Assyria, and I will return them to their homes, declares the Lord. (Hos 11:8–11)

Here at last, we see love's *hurt* and love's *hope*. It is amazing to realize that God, as an expression of his love for us, allows us to affect him. By his love he refuses to be distant and removed from our pain. The picture of the suffering servant in Isaiah is of one who is wounded for our transgressions (Isa 53:5). He is intimately affected by us. If we seek to find a unity in the love of God in Christ, we must let the lives of others affect us. In some circumstances, we may not be able to remove another's pain. We may even be convinced that their struggle will continue as they pursue the course that they are on. But we can still let it affect us. After all, patience

---

3. Allison, *Cruelty of Heresy*.

is not mere tolerance. To tolerate is to refuse to allow something to get to you. But patience is very different. Its definition is in the word itself: long-suffering. Not only do we let it get to us (suffering), but we let it do so over extended periods (long). Tolerance is the fruit of the Stoics. Patience is the fruit of the Holy Spirit.

This in turn leads us to love's *hope* and love's *future*. Do we actually believe that we have one? When we consider where we go from here in this Anglican/Episcopal mess in which we find ourselves, do we really believe that God can bring us to a place of unity? My best answer is yes, but only with much prayer. We must pray with one another and for one another. This of course requires our having those with whom we disagree actually *come to mind*. Even to heart. To pray for someone is not the same as praying about them. Pray *for* them. Develop a plan. In my daily devotions I have a method for praying for every group with whom I have served. This alone takes me into about every battlefield in this fight! Let God bring people to our minds, all sorts and conditions of people to our minds. Choose to love them, in prayer, before God.

To be perfectly frank, we are in a very difficult place in the Anglican Communion. A perilous road lies ahead. Theology matters. Doctrine matters. We are dealing with what we understand of what God has chosen to reveal to us about himself, his nature, his character, and his ways. There is only one environment in which we can hammer out an understanding of God that keeps us from being at one another's throats. There is a unity that is greater than doctrine. It is the unity of God's love in Christ.

7

The Tragedy of Communion
—Dorsey W. M. McConnell

O God the Father of our Lord Jesus Christ, our only Savior, the Prince of Peace: Give us grace seriously to lay to heart the great dangers we are in by our unhappy divisions; take away all hatred and prejudice, and whatever else may hinder us from godly union and concord; that, as there is but one Body and one Spirit, one hope of our calling, one Lord, one Faith, one Baptism, one God and Father of us all, so we may be all of one heart and one soul, united in one holy bond of truth and peace, of faith and charity, and may with one mind and mouth glorify thee; through Jesus Christ our Lord. Amen.[1]

SAYING "NO" TO A SPIRIT OF DIVISION: A PERSONAL INTRODUCTION

I WAS RAISED AN Episcopalian, was smitten by Christ's sovereign grace in my baptism at the age of five, ran from God as hard as I could during my adolescence, and was brought back to him by degrees through influences as disparate as Russian Orthodoxy, the

---

1. Episcopal Church, *Book of Common Prayer*, 818.

poetry of John Donne and George Herbert, Catholic socialism, and evangelical theologians such as C. S. Lewis and John Stott. It was in a remarkable Charismatic parish on the Upper West Side of Manhattan that I came face-to-face with Christ crucified and risen, acknowledged him as my Savior and Lord, and pledged myself to him forever. Above all, the long-suffering grace and mercy God showed me through the love of my wife Betsy and my son Evan persuaded me that God's good news is as good as he says it is.

At some point in 1997, during my tenure as rector of Saint Alban's Church in the Seattle area, I became so disillusioned with the leadership of The Episcopal Church (TEC) that I seriously contemplated leaving the denomination. I remember well the blend of sadness, hurt, anger, and resolve, but for some reason I had what I can only call a check in my spirit, a nameless reservation that gnawed at me from deep inside. At that point, I drove across to the East Side to have my weekly prayer session with my friend Bishop R. E. Taylor. Bishop Taylor pastored a mainly African American Pentecostal church in Bellevue; he and I had been praying together weekly since shortly after the Promise Keepers Pastors Conference in Atlanta in 1995, a relationship that we maintained for seven more years until I was called to Boston. I trusted Richard, and I needed his counsel. He was even more conservative than I (he once noted that, even more than the crazy things Episcopalians were doing with sex, his main concern was that we were what he called "wine-bibbers"). I felt certain he would break through my ambivalence and help me get out the door once and for all.

I poured out my heart in his study, and he listened quietly. When I finished, he sighed, pointed to the shelved volumes of theology and Scripture next to his desk, and said, "Brother, reach me down that big book all the way up top." I got up and retrieved a tome the size of a New York City phone book. On the spine were the words: "Directory of African American Denominations." I sat down and began leafing through it. Richard said, "Go ahead and just read me something." So I did. I cannot remember the exact entry, so what follows, and the details of Richard's response, are approximations, but what I read was something like this: "Full

A House Divided?

Gospel Holiness Tabernacle of God in Jesus Christ (Northern Iowa)." Richard looked into the distance, nodded his head, and said: "Oh, Northern Iowa. Yes, yes, yes. Now, I remember what happened there. You see, the presenting issue was an accusation that Bishop Johnson had abandoned the claim that the gift of tongues was necessary and sufficient evidence of Baptism in the Holy Ghost. But actually, there was a whole lot more going on; see, his former sister-in-law's stepfather had a big church on the other side of town where a lot of Bishop Johnson's people had gone after they left years earlier because of his divorce? So then . . ." What followed was a narrative in which ego and power were so intertwined with doctrine and authority, I held my breath like a child listening to a ghost story. When he finished, there was a pause. Finally he said, "You want to read me something else?" I shook my head, and I asked, "You mean there is a story like that behind each one of these?" He said, "Yes, mostly. Some not as bad, others a whole lot worse, but it all comes down to the same thing. You see, brother," and here he leaned very close and looked straight at me, "when a spirit of division enters the Body of Christ, it just keeps dividing. And dividing. And dividing. Until somebody says no."

I'll never forget the drive back to my parish; it was a rare sunny afternoon in January in Seattle and the mountains were putting on a show, but all I could think of was how completely I had just been changed. I knew my call was to say no to the spirit of division and bear the cost of it, even if some of that cost was a part of my own conscience. I figured that if I was eventually thrown out of TEC, that would be a different matter, but that I would do everything I could to preserve the unity of the Church. That evening at our regular Wednesday Eucharist, as I gazed at the Priest's Host in my hands, I had what was not exactly a vision, but what was a whole lot more than an assurance, what I can only describe as a personal revelation. I saw that the Church was not a thing, an object that could be cut up and repackaged by human will. I saw what is the most obvious fact, that she is the bride of Christ, and his body visible on earth, and that although she is shattered across nearly countless institutional varieties and brands, she is mystically preserved by the sovereignty of the Father as One, Holy, Catholic, and Apostolic.[2] In the moment that I broke the bread, I saw that communion is no mere sign of polity that can be regulated, declared, or rescinded by bishops or councils, but a mystery that is truly and literally the One Church's share in the death and resurrection of the Son. The unity of the Church therefore exists in the Father's very heart and can only no longer exist by the Son's judgment alone.

I know this is a rather dramatic beginning, but theology done at the heart of the Church is far more like drama than it is like science, and that is what we are doing when we pursue the restoration of Christian unity: theology at the heart of the Church, amid her yearnings and her failures, her glories and her humiliations. That is in part why I have called this address "The Tragedy of Communion," because all good drama, including the Bible, has a cast; in this case, it is we who are the cast, all of us who make up the Church, and the Church is, among other things, an extension of that biblical cast in time and history, seeking to make sense of the apostolic witness to the cross and resurrection of Jesus, to embody that witness in our lives, and to deal faithfully with the catastrophes that occur when radically different interpretations of this mystery collide, mix with other social and intellectual forces, and tear the visible Church asunder.

A DIVIDED CHURCH AND A DIVIDED TABLE

Our present divisions are nowhere more apparent than at the eucharistic table, and this is one reason I have chosen to call communion a tragedy. The experience of the tragedy of communion as it plays out in a divinity school where Episcopal and other Anglican students share space and time is complicated, but looks something like this. Some individuals who are members of TEC do not receive the Eucharist from priests affiliated with the Anglican Church in North America (ACNA) or the Province de l'Eglise

---

2. Ibid., 854.

A House Divided?

Anglicane au Rwanda en USA (PEAR-USA), and vice versa; Reformed Episcopal Church (REC) individuals do not receive from women or TEC clergy. Others do not receive communion from one another as a witness to the "gravity of our divisions," because the denominations are in litigation with one another, because their bishops have told them not to receive, or due to personal conviction. Some do not receive because there are "openly gay" persons in your community. There are also many of you who receive from all. Since most seminarians are younger, members of a so-called "post-conflict" generation, this complicates the divisions. Many did not participate in active discernment about whether to remain in TEC or begin attending an ACNA parish, but they grew up or came to the Lord or found Jesus in these places not thinking of them as anything more or less than home. When these future priests and teachers see someone shrink back from them at the Lord's table, or feel that they themselves must shrink back, I know no better term for this than "tragedy." And while I know that most seminarians have not been embroiled in the conflicts of the recent past, they will certainly have conflicts of their own over the next thirty years or so. They will find that the tensions they began to feel while in seminary, and the questions of how, and to what extent, to embrace another who claims the name of Christ but doesn't fit their understanding of what that should look like, will be just as nettlesome, perhaps more so, as they practice leadership in their particular corners of a multifarious Church in a pluralistic world.

With all this in mind, I want to explore the nature of unity and disunity, theologically and scripturally, through four questions. First, how does the New Testament guide and move, push and restrain us as we contemplate remaining in or breaking communion within the visible Church? Here I will look briefly at texts from the epistles that are often thought to be about breaking unity, and then turn to the parable of the wheat and the tares. Second, what is the deep nature of the Church's unity that (I say) is in the heart of the Father; does it really exist, how has it come about, how does it endure, how is it broken? This is a compound question, of course, but I find the Gospel of John often yields compound questions, and the High Priestly Prayer of John 17 (which I will examine next) is no exception. Third, under what conditions, if any, might the *visible disunity* of Christ's body *actually amount to broken communion in the heart of the Father*? Here I will consider two significant splits: the fourth-century Donatist controversy and the twentieth-century Confessing Church movement born from the Barmen Declaration, in which the very nature of the Church was at stake. Fourth and finally, *what ought our actions* and attitudes to be toward one another in light of what we have discovered through these questions? What sort of relationship can we hope for in the future, not only between TEC and ACNA but across the Anglican Communion, and what parts might we be called to play in what I will dare to call a drama of redemption?

AN OBLIGATION TO WITHDRAW?

There are a few New Testament texts that allude to separating from a brother or sister who is in sin and unrepentant: it seems that the events justifying such separation would have to be public and dangerous to the body (such as the "immoral man" living with his father's wife in 1 Cor 5:1, or the one stirring up division in Titus 3:10). The more consistent concern across the epistles, however, is the question of how to respond to "false teachers" who are seen as not merely annoying but destructive. The content of their teaching varies but in different ways strikes at the heart of the gospel of grace. The itinerant teachers in 2 John who "do not confess that Jesus Christ has come in the flesh" (2 John 1:7) seem to be denying the humanity of the Lord. For Jude, the trouble is from "those who pervert the grace of our God into sensuality and deny our only master and Lord, Jesus Christ" (Jude 1:4). This seems to be the Corinthian story in another guise: limitless grace means we can sin as much as we want. Its explicit echoes in 2 Peter 2:1–2 indicate that it must have been a popular brand: sort of a prosperity gospel with sex at the center and representing (in a way we are not told) a major income stream for the preacher, since "greed" is apparently a primary complaint. In Galatia, the teachers are of a different variety, preaching a harsh and syncretistic legalism that also insisted on circumcision (Gal 5:1–6, and throughout the letter). Again and again these epistles warn of the "destructive" power of such teachers, and urge that they be avoided (as in Titus), rebuked, cut off (as in Galatians), or not welcomed (as in 2 John).

Concluding from all this that one had the obligation to withdraw from a Church that had (in the eye of the beholder) become dominated by such people certainly cannot be considered unreasonable. You shouldn't need a sign from heaven telling you to get out of the way of danger when the train is bearing down on you, and the urgency is even greater if you are standing on the tracks with your children. Protestant denominations going back to the Reformation have used just this reasoning in some of their founding documents. Nonetheless, it is interesting that so many of these texts stop short of saying that if you can't get false teachers out of the Church, you have to pull the Church away from the false teachers. In fact many of them go in the opposite direction: endure, be patient, be spotless, build yourselves up in faith, keep yourselves in the love of God, have mercy on those who doubt. And the reason for what I will call this theology of patient endurance seems to lie in something all the writers see in the supernatural nature of the Church and her unity. Nowhere does Paul suggest that a church is no longer the Church merely because parts of it are under the influence of false teachers, and nowhere it seems to me does he give permission for half a congregation leaving First Baptist to start Second Baptist. Rather Paul insists that those who bear the name of Christ, even in the swamp of arrogance and irreligion that makes up much of the Church in Corinth, are to hold onto one another in that swamp for dear life, as hands that cannot do without feet, ears that cannot do without eyes, inalienable members of the same body (1 Cor 12:14–27), which is nothing other than the mystical body of Christ.

The delicacy of this deep interconnectedness across all the members of the body, even in our sin, is nowhere more clearly expounded than in the parable of the wheat and the tares (Matt 13:24–30). Jesus tells this parable as a warning to the Matthean community that any attempt at the separation of "the righteous" from those "guilty of lawlessness" must wait till the final judgment, because an attempt to save the good fruit by means of separating out the bad fruit may kill good fruit along with bad. On its face (according to the passage interpreting it, Matt 13:36–40) this begins as a parable about a righteous Church in the midst of an evil world, but in verse 41, the Lord makes clear he is also speaking about "causes of sin and all law-breakers" who are to be "gathered out of the kingdom," which only makes sense if they are already present in the Church. Even if we could all agree on who exactly are meant here by the lawless, we are enjoined from separating them out and (I think) similarly enjoined from separating ourselves out *en masse* into a purified community, because of the harm that it might do to the fabric of the Church and hence to the integrity of the gospel. As further evidence of the harm, I invite you to Pittsburgh.

Six years ago, the Episcopal Diocese of Pittsburgh consisted of seventy-six parishes. We now have thirty-seven; our census is slightly more than half what it was before the split. Though there are signs we are growing again, and though I am consistently beginning to hear more excitement for the future than grief over the past, still every Sunday as I visit our parishes I walk through the smoke and blood of the aftermath: the scars of divided congregations, broken relationships, strained finances, compromised witness, even children kept from their friends. I know that many of those who left the diocese mourn this state of affairs nearly as much as those who remained. I also know the decision to leave for many of them was personally agonizing and very costly; in many cases, I am sure they wrestled even more than I did in my decision to stay. Though I am grieved by their choice, I refuse to condemn them for it. Conscience is rightly powerful, and in the end each of us must work out his or her own salvation with fear and trembling (Phil 2:12). And yet, as horrible as the consequences have been, I do not believe the wounds we bear are the most important reason for Jesus warning us not to tear apart the Church. I believe he tells us we *should not* tear the Church because we *cannot* tear the Church.

A House Divided?

THE CHURCH'S UNITY IN THE HEART OF GOD THE FATHER

And that brings me to the second (or compound) question: what is the deep nature of the Church's unity? Does it really exist, how has it come about, how does it endure, how is it broken? In the High Priestly Prayer in John 17, Jesus prays clearly that the Church be one: that as the Son and the Father are one, the Church be perfectly one, "as you, Father, are in me and I am in you, may they also be in us . . . I in them and you in me, that they may become completely one" (John 17:21, 23). Note that this unity is both eternal and invisible (that is, in the very heart of God) and yet also intended to be temporal and visible, revealed in the present, with a particular purpose in showing the world that Jesus is the one sent by the Father (this in two verses, 21 and 23). So Jesus prays for unity, perfect unity, unity both visible and invisible, unity now.

Now, I believe that what Jesus wants, Jesus gets. Any notion that the Father would refuse to honor the prayer of the Son is ridiculous on its face, as is the thought that human agency could disrupt what the Father and the Son have agreed upon. So the only conclusion must be, as I learned at the altar years ago on that sunny winter day in Seattle, that at least in the Father's heart, and in her infinite and eternal mystery, the Church *is* one. Beyond any differences in denominations, beyond her strife, beyond our attempts to distinguish between real presence or spiritual presence, premillennialism or postmillennialism, scriptural authority or biblical inerrancy or papal infallibility, beyond the Augsburg Confession, or the Thirty-Nine Articles, or the Lausanne Covenant, beyond any and all of these she is one, already, in the heart of the Father. This Church has come about through the prayer of the Son, endures through the will of the Father, and can only be broken (as I previously noted) by Jesus himself. The necessary conclusion, I believe, is that we share in that invisible communion beyond our visible differences. So though I may refuse to receive the Host from a priest who is my enemy—that is, who I think to be on the wrong side of a line I think is definitive, and who may return the favor in their attitude toward me—John 17 compels us to consider the possibility, even the likelihood, that we are nonetheless one in the Father's heart, whether or not a Host passes from their hand to mine. That is the possible extent of the invisible and eternal communion Jesus prays for, felt in time and space, that my enemy and I are one, because Christ has chosen us both. And if that is true, then that is a tragedy, in the deepest sense, meaning the result of a story that could not turn out any other way, no matter how desperately we tried to engineer a different outcome, since the outcome was destined, fixed in the heart of the Father from the moment when Jesus opened his hands in prayer in the upper room. And if it is true that what Jesus wants, Jesus gets, this unity of the Church which is in the Father's heart must at least occasionally be spiritually visible to the world even in the midst of our divisions. Surely in a divinity school where Episcopal and other Anglican students experience the journey into ministry together, we should not be surprised that the Father wants to manifest the spiritual unity of the Church in his heart even in the midst of our differences, binding us together across the chasms among and between us without actually getting rid of the chasms themselves, and somehow that he wants to show that unity to the world in a way that lets the world believe Jesus is the one whom the Father has sent. I will return to one particular experience of this in my conclusion.

SEARCHING FOR THE BOUNDARIES OF UNITY

If the spiritual, eternal communion of the body of Christ is a reality, and the corollary is true, that such a communion can only be broken by its author, by Jesus himself, is there a point at which the Church on earth shows signs that Jesus has broken that communion, a point beyond which, though she maintain catholic sacraments and even catholic creeds, she is in fact no longer one with the Church that is in the Father's heart? Certainly we have to explore that possibility, since some in the current controversies that trouble us all have insisted that is exactly what is at stake, that

A House Divided?

TEC came to, and surpassed, just that point in August of 2003, and that separation from TEC, therefore, is not separation from a Church, but simply recognition that what once was part of the mystical body of Christ, is no longer, that Jesus has in fact broken communion with us, in the heart of the Father. On the other hand, there is also a progressive version of the same claim, suggesting that as the Church denies a particular idea of justice and inclusion, it denies Jesus and walks away from God, with the implication that God will have nothing to do with such a church. If that is the claim, then are there other similar crucial moments in Christian history which might give us an idea as to whether the claim has any validity? What we are heading into here is ground for at least a dozen good doctoral dissertations that would look at the history of division more broadly than my friend Bishop Taylor's directory of Christian strife. But perhaps there are two salient instances of churches with terrible symptoms in this regard that we might briefly consider and then ask what they might teach us.

At one end of history lies the Donatist controversy. At the beginning of the fourth century, during the two-year persecution under the Roman emperor Diocletian, Christians (and especially their clergy) were required on pain of death to renounce their faith in public and remit to local authorities the treasures of the Church as a sign of their sincerity. While the persecution was particularly intense in Rome, it was enforced with varying degrees of enthusiasm elsewhere by provincial governors who frankly had other things to worry about and didn't like to work very hard anyway. This appears to have been the case in North Africa, where the prevailing point of view held that the sea was wide and Rome was far away. In these districts it was thought to be enough for clergy to hand over the Church's Scriptures and pay a fine. Eventually, the persecution passed, and life would have gone on as before had it not been for a large minority of Christians who objected that clergy who had acquiesced to the state's demands were apostate, even after they repented, and that no sacraments (including Baptism) celebrated at their hands could possibly be valid. Note that this argument, in effect, said that the Church, though catholic in form, was not Church in reality, because its ministers had sinned. It was Augustine's famous argument that the efficacy of the sacrament inhered in the work itself (*ex opere operato*), not in anything to do with the character of the minister, which eventually carried the day, in effect turning the tables on the Donatists. Augustine insisted that by denying the full extent of God's sovereign grace, by setting limits on the operation of grace rooted in the fallibility of the clergy, the Donatists denied that God's salvation could reach to anyone in need in spite of the defective spiritual state of the one chosen as bearer of that grace. In other words, if I tell Jesus he can't have a sheep he wants because his under-shepherds aren't clean, I am not only describing a boundary to the Church that does not exist in the heart of the Father; I am also standing on the wrong side of the line I have just described.

At the other end, in our own time, we might consider the circumstances that gave birth to the Confessing Church in Nazi Germany, the great opposing force to the so-called "German Christians." Here again, interestingly enough, the core issues are salvation and sacrament, again particularly the sacrament of Baptism. By 1935, the true horror of Nazism had established an overwhelming influence in many of the Protestant churches. Essential to their proclamation was the contention that Jews who had been baptized were no more part of the Church than they had been before, and further, that it was Aryan blood, not Baptism, that made one both a Christian and a German. The true extent of this evil may be read in a jingle hung on a signboard in Westphalia, "Die Taufe mag ganz nützlich sein / Doch glattet sie kein Nasenbein" [Baptism may be quite useful, but it cannot straighten out a nose].[3] Again, as in the Donatist controversy, the "German Christians" sought to establish a "pure church" through an unbiblical limit to the sacrament of Baptism. Admittedly the notion of "purity" at issue here was radically different from that of the Donatists, drawing from the power of the State rather than opposing it, but the end result was similar: they drew a boundary to the Church which clearly did not exist in

---

3. Bergen, *Twisted Cross*, 86.

A House Divided?

the heart of the Father, and wound up ironically on the wrong side of the line they themselves drew. The theologian Karl Barth and his friends pointed out exactly this in establishing the Confessing Church movement in the Barmen Declaration of 1934.

Both of these have resonances for us in our recent controversies. I have heard some of my more progressive friends in TEC sometimes talk as if the separation of "the other side" reflects a delusional quest for purity, a kind of Donatist rigorism, and hence a church that is not Church. Similarly, there are some on the other side who have suggested that TEC is not a church because in their view though we may observe catholic form and sacraments, in reality we have surrendered ourselves to modern secular culture the way the Reich Church surrendered to German culture of the 1930s and 1940s, and some have explicitly read that suggestion into some key language of their movement such as the Fellowship of Confessing Anglicans (FCA) and the Jerusalem Declaration. Obviously, I think both of these characterizations are as unhelpful as they are untrue, the sort of hyperbole generated in a messy divorce, not the language of a considered ecclesiology. Furthermore we may clearly note that in both cases, that of the Donatists and that of the Reich Church, it is not Jesus who is drawing the boundary to break his communion, but rather only human leaders. In fact we may infer that Jesus refuses to break communion in either instance: I believe in the end that Augustine actually asserts that heaven quite likely would include his old opponents, or at least many of them, and I believe the same is true (though it is harder for us to digest culturally) of the German Christians.[4] I cannot of course prove it, but I strongly suspect that if John 17 is true, then the Father, tireless in his love, is also consistent and passionate in extending the Church of his heart, the One Church that exists, across all the lines we draw against it.

I believe this with all my heart, and yet I know that to make this reality more and more visible, there are of course huge

---

4. Only 10 percent of Christians in Germany actually joined the Confessing movement, but I am sure thousands of others worked quietly to subvert the racism of the state through their churches in other ways.

institutional questions that face our fragmented Anglican churches going forward. These questions have the usual ramifications around money and real estate and power and even post-colonial global politics. However, I believe we have a call to address them as if the eternal unity of the Church could actually become a temporal reality. In the Diocese of Pittsburgh, even in the midst of division, we have no active litigation, nor has the diocese ever sued a parish. We have never deposed a priest for leaving TEC, releasing them instead under the non-disciplinary Title III of our canons. We are in good-faith dialogue with a number of ACNA congregations concerning the properties they occupy. While I cannot speak for anyone beyond the Diocese of Pittsburgh, were we to move further toward questions of institutional reconciliation between our churches, whatever that might eventually look like, we would hope for a sincere effort on both sides to address some key problems. Speaking only for myself, I would hope that the leadership of ACNA at some point might come to the point at which they can publicly state that they view TEC as a Christian Church and as a constituent member of the Anglican Communion and that they renounce their intention to supplant us as a "replacement jurisdiction." There are several other elements I would personally like to see in place, but these would be a good place to start.

I am under no illusions regarding how difficult this kind of institutional reconciliation will be. It is unlikely that we will make much progress during my tenure as bishop: ten years (twelve at the outside) is a drop in the bucket as time is figured in the Church. But our God is the Lord of the Unlikely (if he weren't, I wouldn't be Bishop of Pittsburgh!), and he calls us to live out the vocation of this cross in as many ways as we can. That is why *institutional reconciliation* must be preceded by *relational reconciliation*, and relational reconciliation is slow, painstaking, and painful. It means reaching out your hand a dozen times and having it slapped away, but continuing to do so, no matter how often you are rejected. It means crossing lines the person on the other side does not believe can or should be crossed, and doing so in love. It means finding small ways to bridge enormous chasms: a meal here, a beer there, a Bible study, a prayer group, a common outreach or mission effort, a pastoral visit to someone in need who did not suspect you believed you were their brother or sister in Christ. Through such things in Pittsburgh we are laying one by one the foundation stones of reconciliation, hoping that our children and grandchildren will build upon them.

When imagining processes of institutional and relational reconciliation, participants often call for the interactions between the disputants to take place on neutral ground. However, as we imagine and pray for a future in which the Church as Christ's body is visibly reconciled, I would ask that we never use that phrase again. There is nothing neutral about the love of Calvary. Ephraim Radner in his book *A Brutal Unity* has reminded us that the love within the Church, our love for each other, is and has always been the love of the enemy.[5] The seminary is the laboratory where priests begin to practice that love, whether they know it or not, because the Father is practicing it in them and through them as he seeks to join all of them more deeply to the one Church that is in his heart. And the rest of the Church desperately needs the witness of leaders who have learned to love in this way. I know nothing I have said will solve the ongoing difficulties of how seminarians celebrate or receive communion. But I will offer one final story and one final testimony which may help to illustrate how God may be made powerfully manifest in these difficulties.

Sometime in the early 1970s there was a Roman Catholic missionary who had worked for years in Amazonia. He had built a strong and populous indigenous Catholic community, and one day the people said to him, "Today we will go down the river to visit our cousins. We would like you to come along." The priest knew this was a great honor and represented a major advancement in his relationship with his people; so he went with them. Their canoes traveled a full day, and when they finally arrived at the village, the priest immediately noticed the hamlet was built around a large open hut with a cross over it. This, too, was a Christian village, and

---

5. Radner, *Brutal Unity*.

their white pastor greeted the priest as he stepped onshore. He was a minister of the Reformed Church. Immediately the two realized they had a potential problem on their hands, and retired discreetly to talk. Within five minutes they had arrived at a solution. They agreed that, when visiting the Protestant village, the priest would preach, and the pastor would celebrate the Lord's Supper according to the ordinance of the Reformed Church; and similarly, when the party was in the Catholic village, the pastor would preach and the priest would say Mass.

This all worked very well until word got back to the authorities in Sao Paulo, and two directives eventually came down for the clergy to cease and desist. After struggling with his conscience for a good while, the priest wrote to the Franciscan theologian Leonardo Boff, and eventually he received this reply:

> My dear Father; I have read your letter. Here is my counsel: The time has grown very short, and the kingdom of God is at hand. Therefore if you are in the presence of a Christian community whose leader has been set apart by prayer and the laying on of hands for a ministry of Word and Sacrament, the Lord's Supper he celebrates is the Eucharist. We can no longer allow Christ's little ones to trip over the stumbling blocks of the sixteenth century.[6]

I know there are times this is more easily said than done. There is a wonderful ministry to the homeless in Pittsburgh called Shepherd's Heart. It is run by Father Mike Wurschmidt, who is quite simply one of the godliest men I know. Mike left the Episcopal Diocese to join ACNA during the split, but this ministry remained dear to hundreds of people across the divide, and his board includes folks on both sides. The Diocese managed to settle the property issue to everyone's benefit, and fourteen of our parishes continue in partnership with Shepherd's Heart. About a year ago, I visited with a group of our youth to help out on a Sunday night. Mike celebrated the Eucharist and preached to a crowd of mixed TEC and ACNA volunteers, lay and clergy. At the invitation

---

6. Although attributed to Leonardo Boff, the provenance of this anecdote is uncertain.

to communion I got up with everybody else and began to come forward; I was halfway down the aisle, caught up in a praise song when it caught up to me. "Holy Cow," I thought, "he is an ACNA priest, and I am the freaking Episcopal Bishop of Pittsburgh!" I realized after a few seconds that I didn't know what was going on here, I didn't know the deacons ministering with Mike, and I didn't want him to get into any trouble, so the best thing was for me to cross my arms and ask for his blessing, which I did. And together we held onto each other for a couple of minutes and prayed together for the unity of the Church. When I went back to my seat, I saw all of my clergy and laity were receiving from him, and I heaved a sigh of relief that I had not been a stumbling block. But there was more.

When I called Mike to ask his permission to tell this story, I was driving around the airport parking lot in Pittsburgh looking for a space, and I told him what I just wrote here, and he agreed that it was powerful, and just the way he remembered, but then he said, "Yeah, and I will never forget what happened next." I said, "What do you mean?" He said, "What you did." I paused. I was driving up and down the aisles looking for a space that didn't exist and now I was trying to come up with a memory that wasn't there. "What did I do?" I asked. He said, "You fell to your knees and put your hands up and began to weep, and I knew you were praying for our wounded Church." I slammed on the brakes, put the car in park, and burst into tears. I could see myself there in my mind's eye, but I honestly don't know if that is because it happened and I was remembering it, or because I was seeing what Mike saw that night, seeing with him the Church in the heart of the Father, seeing the spiritual unity manifest even in the midst of our troubles. I wept into the phone, and I said, "Mike, these are the tears of Peter; may our Lord be merciful to us." And we prayed for a couple more minutes. (And, yes, after I regained my composure, Mike prayed I would find a parking space; I drove about a hundred feet farther and there it was.)

I promised finally to give you a little counsel about how you might proceed here as you continue to build your common life, and so my last comments will point that way. I said earlier that the Church needs you, but that is not all. The fact is that I need you. Here you can do things that I cannot. You have liberty here that I do not, a liberty I need to know you are using generously and well. When I as bishop must cross my arms and not receive the Host, I pray as I am being blessed that my Lord will not cross his arms when I am presented to him to be received in the last day. And while I would not have you be disobedient to your bishops or to your conscience, I would hope that you might be as charitable to one another in your table fellowship as God in Christ has been to you. And at the time of Communion, if you cannot receive, for any reason, might you by twos or threes fall to your knees and pray for the healing and unity of our wounded Church? As you do so, how might the Father of lights manifest through you, to Our Lord's little ones, the fullness of the glory of the body of Christ which is and finally shall be one?

> O God of unchangeable power and eternal light: Look favorably on your whole Church, that wonderful and sacred mystery; by the effectual working of your providence, carry out in tranquility the plan of salvation; let the whole world see and know that things which were cast down are being raised up, and things which had grown old are being made new, and that all things are being brought to their perfection by him through whom all things were made, your Son Jesus Christ Our Lord; who lives and reigns with you, in the unity of the Holy Spirit, one God, for ever and ever. Amen.[7]

---

7. Episcopal Church, *Book of Common Prayer*, 280.

8

Responses

Sacramental Relationality

—Bryan Biba

While certainly admirable, the aim of these "fierce conversations" was initially unclear to me. As our conversations progressed, the reasons for my lack of clarity became increasingly clear: so many things divide our two provinces, indeed our entire Communion. How could we possibly have a single "fierce conversation" about our divisions without having numerous fierce *conversations* about the Eucharist, gender identity and sexuality, biblical hermeneutics, ecclesial authority, and theological anthropology—just to name a few topics. Such disagreements cut across denominational lines, dividing nearly every congregation in both TEC and ACNA.

But even if we could address each of these topics (perhaps through another series of evening discussions), they would still miss something. Regardless of what we may personally believe or collectively decide on, the conflicts within Anglicanism are beyond our control. As many of our speakers stressed, the decisions of our bishops precede many of our calls to ministry or even our involvement in the Anglican Communion.

Throughout our conversations, all of us were reminded of an important yet difficult point: theological truth does not exist in a vacuum; we are both partially *shaped by* and *accountable to* our context. This is a point Anglicanism in particular has historically defended since the Protestant Reformation. Against the perceived "tyrannical universalizing" tendencies of the Roman Catholic Church, the Church of England emphasized the need for contextually sensitive ministry that could flexibly adapt to language and culture. Yet against many radical Protestants, Anglicans defended the need for order and tradition as a living deposit of ecclesial responses to the crises of the day.

In late modernity, many Christians resonate with these classically Anglican sentiments. Some desire a connection to the past that will save them from their scandalous sense of particularity, which unchecked often leads to blind nostalgia. Others demand honesty concerning our historical limits and hope such intellectual integrity leads to revisionist enlightenment and liberation from "meaningless traditions." Still other Christians assert our utter captivity to human history and culture, thus validating our cultural surrender to nihilistic pluralism.

All these perspectives fall prey to a common late-modern temptation: the reduction of all truth to culture and history. And because of its historical commitment to "contextualized traditioning" (Ellen Davis) or "local catholicity" (Bruce Kaye), Anglicanism is particularly vulnerable to this late-modern temptation. If history is determined by the random whims of uncontrollable forces of culture, then the Church is tragically subject to fate. Jesus' promise that "the gates of hell shall not prevail against [her]" (Matt 16:18) must be false—the wishful thinking of an idealistic ancient writer.

I confess that I often entertain this possibility in moments of weakness; yet in the midst of such doubts, we must remember the Church's confession. Christians do not believe in the shadow of fate or the *Geist* of human progress but in the Holy Spirit "who has spoken through the prophets" and who will "guide us into all truth" (John 16:13). And if the Spirit of God is *the* Lord of history, then

A House Divided?

our Lord Jesus Christ is the basis and safeguard of the Church's unity.

At this trying time of division, when our communion is threatened by the late-modern temptation, Anglicans need to remember to whom the Church and her history belong. I was encouraged to hear each of our contributors affirm the absolute unbreakability of the Church in spite of her members' attempts to tear apart the body. Even in the midst of doubt and the reality of the Church's all-too-public failures, we must continue to be the Church—and we must begin with one another.

Indeed, while we presently have little control over the current conflicts, we do have a great deal of power in this space, this Anglican Episcopal House of Studies. Each of our speakers commented on the unique opportunities for reconciliation our community provides. We are not under the authority of any bishop. Our worship is community governed and community led. As part of an ecumenically minded United Methodist divinity school, we regularly welcome persons from beyond the Anglican tradition. As Bishop McConnell put it, AEHS is an anomaly, a happy anomaly.

The most critical questions going forward deal with the nature of our community. What is this peculiar liminal space the Lord has called us to? What is our unique witness to a Church in the throes of conflict? How should we order our common life to embody the reconciliation we long to see within our local communities and our worldwide Communion? What kinds of ministers does the Anglican Communion need in the twenty-first century?

AEHS at Duke Divinity School has two particular charisms our divided Communion desperately needs. If we as a community embrace these two interrelated gifts, we will be a powerful witness to the larger Church as we seek to heal our "impaired communion."

1. Relationality

Anglicanism is a Communion of churches. Its contours are defined by our relationships. Our communion is weakened when we do not talk to one another, when we settle for stereotypes and generalizing narratives of the other. AEHS serves as a witness to communion when we engage interpersonally with those with whom we disagree.

2. Sacramental Worship

Anglicanism's commitment to relationality goes beyond personal relationships, because communion is greater than the sum of its parts. Our daily worship strengthens our relationships by incorporating us into Christ by the power of the Holy Spirit. This is why we must follow the advice of our speakers and continue to pray together.

Through communal performance of these spiritual gifts, the members of AEHS will be formed into the kind of leaders our Anglican Communion desperately needs: members of Christ's body who resist the temptations of our late-modern world, persons about whom the world will say, "See how they love one another" (John 13:35).

Gathered at the Foot of the Cross
—Molly McGee Short

In the days preceding each of our conversations with bishops from Episcopal and other Anglican dioceses, I felt a growing sense of dread and foreboding. Our conversations yielded a visceral response within me because each week I came face to face with the ugliness and hatred accompanying our recent schisms. Entering into these conversations was like stepping to the edge of a deep chasm and gazing over the edge to see people and churches broken on its rocks. Each week I crept to the edge to marvel at the seemingly unbridgeable distance between Episcopalians and other Anglicans. Each week tore my heart.

The pain of schism was made even more acute by my flourishing friendships with those on the other side. Our unexpected friendships across the chasm thrived despite our stances on opposite sides of the split, making the pain of schism more terrible.

It was these friendships, fed by our communal prayer, which together prevented me from abandoning or withdrawing from these anxiety-inducing conversations. Our shared prayer life gathers us at the foot of the cross. During Morning Prayer, I have taken to gazing at the crucifix in the front of the chapel. When the rising sun illumines the crucifix, the shadow of Jesus' broken body leans towards us and broods over us. In our prayer, friendships, and conversations, we draw near to our crucified Lord, placing our fingers into the wounds of his broken body: the Church.

These conversations make us very vulnerable to one another because no one has escaped unscathed by our schisms. All have been wounded, and these conversations involve not only probing the wounds of Jesus' body but also letting others probe our own wounds.

For this very reason, we must hold fast to charity in continuing conversations with one another. There is a great temptation within these vulnerable contexts to turn our energies towards tearing holes in one another's arguments, to make others look foolish or heretical. This temptation to belligerent conversation is even more pressing since many of us recently converted, or are rediscovering our zeal for our Episcopal and Anglican roots. But once conversation turns in this direction, it is increasingly difficult to dissipate mounting anger and resentment among us.

Charity does not mean easy fixes or glossing over differences, but it does mean that we forgive and seek forgiveness when we cruelly pin or manipulate one another in our speech. It means acknowledging wounds we inflict on one another, repenting, and forgiving.

So let us continue to pray together, to eat together, and to engage in these difficult conversations together because they are gifts. Looking to our crucified Lord, may the Holy Spirit fill us with courage, hope, and faithfulness to live into our calling to be his body.

A Naïve Hope

—David Wantland

The principal question on which these conversations turned—where do we go from here?—was an important one. Each convener had personal and ecclesial memory, which, paired with gospel and tradition consciousness, helped us imagine faithful ways forward amidst the questions with which our unhappy divisions have presented us.

Worship together, pray together, laugh together. Be patient. Be humble. Be repentant. Love your dissenter. These are all worthwhile exhortations.

Yes, it is a good thing that we talk together about our unhappy divisions, simply because they have happened and there is no Christian recourse but to address their reality and seek reconciliation, whatever shape it takes. And perhaps Bishop Bauerschmidt was right in saying that a rehash is uncalled for. Certainly if by "rehash," he means a reenactment of a vitriolic, polemicized battle over brick, mortar, and moral high ground, I'm in agreement. But as our conversations proceeded Wednesday after Wednesday, I grew more and more certain that, regarding the nature of the split, we have little idea what we are talking about. I think a rehash of sorts may be in order.

Take one example. Supposedly, we all know what the term "practicing homosexual" means. I confess to having no clue what we mean when we us that term. I'd guess that if we scratched the surface of the oft-referenced tropes about the origins of our divisions—absence of episcopal discipline, inconsistency of Scripture with a particular stance on human sexuality, traditional view of scriptural authority—we will confront confusion over Christology, pneumatology, Scripture, Church polity, and more.

So here's a quick scratch. Is it particular genital contact that is proscribed or are disordered desires in view? Has The Episcopal Church (TEC) wrongly adopted the language of orientation essentialism for its discourse? Are the historic "goods of marriage" that are appealed to within the Christian tradition in fact "Christian"? What do we mean by our appeal to episcopal authority or to episcopal discipline? What bearing does Anglican polity have on evaluating the events that precipitated and followed the split(s)? I am convinced that we cannot know where to go from here if we cannot isolate our judicatories' answers to these questions.

So where do we, the Duke Divinity School Anglican Episcopal House of Studies, go from here? Now, no one asked me this question, but I'll take my liberties and give a brief answer here.

I think we need to take up the suggestions of our gracious conveners and continue to pray together, worship together, and laugh together. And out of the relationships that we have cultivated through these practices, we can begin to work anew. We need to make use of the ecclesially ambiguous space we inhabit here and open ourselves to the Spirit and to one another as we struggle to understand what exactly is at the root of our unhappy divisions. It may be naïve to think that there is some chance to redirect the paths our churches now seem set upon. But if this is the last place in which to work out the naïve hope that the Spirit may stir within our respective jurisdictions a movement of mutual recognition and Calvary love, I would nevertheless have us to do it.

Toward a Shared Narrative

—MICHELLE WOLFE HOWARD

In our Anglican-Episcopal conversations we have heard five narratives exploring our past, present, and future. As I listened to these narratives it was striking how different they were, both across and within the Anglican-Episcopal divisions. One major point of divergence in the narratives was the role of human sexuality in the split. While Dean Timothy Kimbrough narrated our division using a timeline of decisions and actions relating to human sexuality, including General Convention decisions and the consecration of Bishop Gene Robinson, sexuality was notably absent from Bishop Terrell Glenn's presentation. What role do such issues as biblical authority, hermeneutics, relationship with the wider Anglican Communion, respecting the authority of bishops, theological liberalism or conservatism, and human sexuality have in the split? In what proportions did they contribute? In the community of the Anglican Episcopal House of Studies, where we have a unique opportunity and witness to the wider Church, I think it essential that we work towards creating a shared narrative of our past in order to understand our present and work towards our future.

I have been particularly grateful for the dinner conversations we had during the dialogues. During that informal time, I had the opportunity to hear others' stories in a way that I had not previously, in order to see similarities and differences with my own narrative. Given that many of us came into the Communion inheriting the decisions of our parishes, we have also inherited particular narratives of struggle, tragedy, and triumphalism. Sharing a narrative does not mean that we flatten our many stories into one, but rather that we acknowledge the truth in each other's experiences and we see how they can fit within and alongside our own. Just as Chronicles and Samuel tell different accounts of Israel's King David, which we nonetheless hold together as truth, there is truth in Episcopal and other Anglican narratives of division, conviction, and disappointment. This narrative-building process requires listening to each other and acknowledging our mutual brokenness. As many presenters suggested, it requires repentance and lament. I hope these informal conversations can continue both in the structures of the House, such as in the listening groups, and outside of them. Until we can share a narrative, it is understandable that we would have trouble sharing a table.

Turning from what has happened to where we go from here, both as a House and as the larger bodies of The Episcopal Church and other Anglican churches in North America, I think it is helpful to discuss the nature of unity using the representations of each presenter. What type of unity do we have now, and what kind of unity can and should we hope towards? Bishop McConnell gave a beautiful account of our unity in the heart of the Father. As long as we acknowledge each other as Christians (which does not often happen across the Episcopal and other Anglican churches in North America), then we acknowledge this unity. If we can agree to this, then the existence of our House has integrity. Standing on our eschatological unity also serves as a foundation for hope in the midst of our communal lament over the divisions we currently experience.

If we have unity in the heart of the Father, then we can ask, like Bishop Glenn, if we have a unity of love. Scale is significant here. Across the Communion, it is clear that we don't have this unity yet. In the House, I present it to you as a topic for debate. Do we exemplify love towards one another? I believe that we can have it here, and that might be the single most powerful witness that AEHS can have in the larger landscape.

Dr. Yates presented gospel unity as a unity that transcends any human structures. He spoke from the assumption that the

A House Divided?

Anglican Churches in North America and TEC do not share a gospel unity, that they hold different conceptions of what the Good News of Jesus is. As students who have been formed together at Duke, a community with a particular telling of the Good News, we have a unique position to work towards this type of unity. The shared words of the creeds can also serve as a foundation for this unity.

Finally, I am not sure how to think of Bishop Bauerschmidt's "Ecumenical Unity" in our context. If our unity should be characterized by ecumenical conversation, then I don't think that AEHS, as a community that worships and lives as one, is a coherent concept. It was notable to me that none of the presenters spoke of unity as characterized through structures. Bishop Bauerschmidt came closest, because firm institutional disunity is a prerequisite for ecumenical unity.

I hope that as we grow to understand each other and our communities, we can recognize the truth in each other's narratives and that our own narratives will stretch and expand to accommodate others' stories as legitimate and important. We can have a shared narrative while recognizing the divisions manifested themselves in particular ways in different communities, congregations, and families. Sharing a narrative is intimately connected to sharing a unity of love with one another—demonstrating our love for each other through listening and valuing each others' dreams, desires, and disappointments. If we can share a narrative of our division, then we are already working towards a shared narrative of our unity, starting with this House.

Because of our common life together in AEHS, we have the opportunity to listen to each other, demonstrating unity in the midst of institutional disunity. May we continue praying, listening, and repenting together as we build a narrative, and a future, that we can share.

9

Homily on Matthew 5:13–20

—David Marshall

You are the salt of the earth; but if salt has lost its taste, how can its saltiness be restored? It is no longer good for anything, but is thrown out and trampled underfoot.

You are the light of the world. A city built on a hill cannot be hid. No one after lighting a lamp puts it under the bushel basket, but on the lampstand, and it gives light to all in the house. In the same way, let your light shine before others, so that they may see your good works and give glory to your Father in heaven.

Do not think that I have come to abolish the law or the prophets; I have come not to abolish but to fulfill. For truly I tell you, until heaven and earth pass away, not one letter, not one stroke of a letter, will pass from the law until all is accomplished. Therefore, whoever breaks one of the least of these commandments, and teaches others to do the same, will be called least in the kingdom of heaven; but whoever does them and teaches them will be called great in the kingdom of heaven. For I tell you, unless your righteousness exceeds that of the scribes and Pharisees, you will never enter the kingdom of heaven.

Matt 5:13–20

A House Divided?

IN OCTOBER 2013, DIRECTOR Robert Orlando released "A Polite Bribe," a documentary about the life of St. Paul, featuring comments by a wide range of New Testament scholars. The film focused chiefly on the tensions between the gospel preached by Paul in his missionary work among Gentiles and the views of those Jewish Christians who were uneasy about Paul's conviction that Gentiles did not have to be circumcised and Torah-observant to become followers of the Messiah. The film came to the conclusion that, after years of simmering tension, James, the leader of the Jewish Christian community in Jerusalem, was relieved to see Paul arrested and taken away by the Roman authorities; indeed it suggested that James instigated Paul's arrest. The tensions in the early Church had become that bad.

I confess I was disturbed. I have long understood that the New Testament churches were not monolithic; there was plenty of diversity, at times disunity, among them. But I had never seen this theme expressed so starkly. While I am aware that the film's conclusions would be regarded as greatly exaggerated by many scholars, nevertheless it reminded me in a salutary way that within the New Testament we have different accounts of Jesus and of the Christian life and that there are some real tensions among them. After watching the film, I read that section of Acts mentioned in it that is rather little known (and certainly not often preached on) where Paul arrives in Jerusalem for the last time. Luke tells us that the Jewish Christian church leaders there say this to Paul: "You see, brother, how many thousands of believers there are among the Jews, and they are all zealous for the law. They have been told about you that you teach all the Jews living among the Gentiles to forsake Moses, and that you tell them not to circumcise their children or observe the customs. What then is to be done? They will certainly hear that you have come" (Acts 21:20–22). We need to hear the nervousness here, the sense of a looming crisis. The Gentile churches taught by Paul are pulling away from the Jewish churches, and the church leaders are trying to find some way of holding things together. They propose that Paul publicly observe certain rituals which will reassure those who are suspicious of him.

In the end it doesn't work; a riot breaks out, Paul is arrested and eventually is taken away to Rome.

The tension in the early Church between Jewish and Gentile approaches to Christian faith and life described at the end of Acts deserves attention, especially as we consider one of the most Jewish moments in the most Jewish of the Gospels, Matthew. This passage from chapter 5 appears nowhere else in the Gospels. Matthew tells us that Jesus says: "Not one letter, not one stroke of a letter, will pass from the law until all is accomplished. Therefore, whoever breaks one of the least of these commandments, and teaches others to do the same, will be called least in the kingdom of heaven" (Matt 5:18–19). If you are a member of the Jewish Christian community in which Matthew's Gospel has been composed, and these are the words of Jesus that your community passes on, what do you think of Paul, this Jew who teaches the Gentiles that they can become part of the Israel of God without obeying all the commandments? What do you think of his extraordinary flouting of the tradition in sayings such as, "Neither circumcision counts for anything, nor uncircumcision, but a new creation . . ." (Gal 6:15)?

With the passage of time, especially after the fall of Jerusalem, the Church would become overwhelmingly Gentile. Paul's message, we could say, won the day. But interestingly, perhaps surprisingly, the writings of Jewish Christian communities such as Matthew's Gospel and the Letter of James were not cast aside. So the New Testament contains both the Pauline gospel, proclaimed in his letters, and the rather different account of the gospel of Christ found in Matthew and also in James. That is the kind of Scripture it has pleased God to give us. Difference was there from the beginning of the story of the Church, at times painful and apparently insuperable difference, generating much anxiety and suspicion. Just as we experience today.

Imagine how impoverished the New Testament would be without Matthew and the texts only he gives us. Without the Beatitudes and the whole Sermon on the Mount; without "Come to me, all you who labor and are heavy laden" (Matt 11:28); without the promise of Jesus to be where two or three are gathered in

A House Divided?

his name; without the Great Commission with which Matthew's Gospel ends. Without Matthew we would not know from today's reading of our vocation to be the salt of the earth and the light of the world. And yet what would Matthew, and those to whom he wrote, have thought of Paul? And of us? Would they see us as proper followers of the Messiah Jesus?

The Church is a complex and fraught reality, with great diversity across time and cultures and the many traditions that have grown within it. It is often hard for us to discern Christ in unfamiliar forms of Christianity. So as we read the New Testament and are enriched in our faith by its many different witnesses, it is salutary to recall the very real tensions that existed between them at times. But if we can trust that in ways beyond our understanding God is at work across the barriers of misunderstanding and suspicion with which we live today, then we can be enriched by the gifts offered to us by God in and through those fellow Christians who are most different from us, and with whom, on some matters, we disagree most deeply.

10

Afterword
A Proposal for the Communion

—WILLIAM GLASS

There are two prisoners, each in their dungeons, who communicate by knocking and knocking against the wall. The wall is what separates them; the wall is what allows their conversation. So it is with us and God. Each separation is a link.[1]

—SIMONE WEIL

THIS BOOK HAS BEEN an attempt to answer the question "Where do we go from here?" in American Anglicanism. Duke Divinity School's Anglican Episcopal House of Studies (AEHS) exists as an experiment—to see if there is a way to negotiate some kind of common life by reaching back into a heritage that both Episcopalians and other Anglicans share. In the wider Communion there are several visions of the future in play at the moment, and while we do not pretend that ours is the only one worth taking seriously,

---

1. Simone Weil, *La Pesanteur et la Grâce*, 164, author's translation.

A House Divided?

we do certainly think there are others on which we would like to foreclose.

First among those is a cut-and-run approach, currently embraced by many of the more strident voices in the Anglican scene, in which those parts of the Communion separated by their views on human sexuality merely cut their losses and move on as if those they had left behind are not Christians. With this approach, we merely draw a wall around the real believers. At times, this wall circles around conservative Anglican bodies in North America and their conservative allies in the Communion's Global South. At others, it encloses liberal Western Anglicans (mainly in the American Episcopal Church and the Anglican Church of Canada) and the See of Canterbury.

While this approach does have the advantage of illustrating differences with a bright line, it has at least one significant problem. That is, whichever way the wall is sketched, it seems unable to rid the landscape of conflict. Conservative Anglicans have attached themselves to various church bodies of the Global South in an attempt to create a new Anglicanism, but they have waged war internally with one another. Liberal Episcopalians have claimed the seal of authenticity conferred upon them by their formal connection to the Archbishop of Canterbury, but they have simultaneously ignored the pastoral guidance of the Communion's foremost See in their own decision-making. If there are enemies within the walls, is it not at least possible that some outside the walls might be surprising friends? By those who have counseled a separatist approach to the intra-Anglican situation, this proposal will doubtless be received with some skepticism; in response, we would only ask how certain such people are that the fruits of the Spirit are no longer to be harvested among their opponents. If the glory has departed, how do they explain what evidence remains of the Spirit's work in those they have left behind?

Another way forward on offer is the communion-without-consensus model that several well-meaning and conciliatory voices have promoted. For these people, the Church-rending conflicts of our day are much ado about nothing. Is there any reason, they wonder, why the Church can't just live around its disagreements over sexuality? But this proposal, for all its good intentions, conceals judgments about the questions that cause the disagreements in the first place. Entailed here are one of two antecedent convictions: either (a) that the practices over which the Church is dividing are not sinful and hence not worth breaking the Church apart (thus begging the whole question again), or (b) that the disagreements are over matters that do not compromise the Church even if there is sin in view. For those who share neither of these assumptions, it is not possible merely to go along. No one who thinks both that homosexual intercourse is sinful and that the Church's members are involved with each other, such that the willful collusion with sin in one part will defile the others, could reasonably be asked to just "live around" those differences. Paul's admonition in 1 Corinthians 5:11 comes to mind here: "You must not associate with anyone who claims to be a brother or sister but is sexually immoral or greedy, an idolater or slanderer, a drunkard or swindler. Do not even eat with such people." She could be asked to change her mind about one or the other of her prior convictions, but that is all.

In the ecclesial space shaped by these two options, there is a distinct danger that Christians on each side of the divide avoid talking to each other at all, or when they do talk they steer away from the difficult issues. But these strategies of avoidance are ultimately untenable. The Church's witness is not advanced by pretending that disagreements (or other Christians) do not exist. There were and are matters of real consequence at stake between us, and it is better that those be recognized and named for what they are. The failure to do so can only lead to disaster for the Communion. For this reason, when Dr. Jo Bailey Wells visited AEHS in the spring semester of 2013 and challenged us to enhance our experiment in intra-Anglican life with "fierce conversations" about the divisions in the Communion, I welcomed the opportunity.

I was an intern for AEHS during the discussions recorded in this book. That meant (for me) showing up early to set up tables for food. It meant shuttling our speakers to their hotels on occasion.

A House Divided?

It meant printing out materials and moving carts and gathering books and staying late to clean up afterward. And it meant viewing in a unique way the "mundane" nature of these events. The grandeur of the topics our speakers addressed and the verve with which they did so might lead those who read the addresses here to forget: these were lectures to students. And as someone who participated in the execution of the details, I know more than most how inadequate a tool these conversations were to achieve the goal we aimed for—wisdom for the road(s) American Anglicanism will take in the future.

And yet, for all the inadequacy of the tool, I also saw over the course of a semester how new possibilities began to open up. I saw people who felt that Anglicanism had reached an impasse catch a glimpse together of a different future, a Church that does not now exist although it may yet. I saw people who assumed (and regretted) that they'd be on opposing sides of a lifelong feud learn to hope that they would not. And, most importantly, I saw people who harbor strong disagreements with one another treat each other with love, with respect, with good faith, and with honor. I attribute much of this grace to the agency of the Holy Spirit acting in ways that would be invisible if one were to note only the words spoken by our guests, inspiring and informative as they were.

AEHS draws together a community of practice whose only condition is the ability to confess together what is contained in the Morning Office of the BCP (insofar as we pray that together each morning). Within AEHS, there are disagreements mirroring nearly all of those found within the Communion. And AEHS requires no prior consensus on these matters. What it does require is a commitment to assume the best about those with whom you disagree, a commitment that is guarded intentionally by prayer and habitual gathering. In my own time at AEHS, I found myself regularly praying for those with whom I disagreed, that God would open their eyes to the truth on some or other question. At times, that happened. At times my prayers for them resulted in my own mind changing. Still other times, disagreements merely remained between us.

Yet we continued to gather and to pray together. The conversations that are reflected in this book continued in small-group gatherings over the course of the semester, groups in which Episcopalians are deliberately placed with other Anglicans. Those groups are obliged, in a process of Anglican Spiritual Formation, to gather regularly for fellowship and conversation. The topics addressed by our speakers provided the fodder for those conversations in the spring of 2014, but the groups had been meeting, praying, disagreeing, and continuing since before then. Over time, those groups developed trust in one another, confidence in each other's good faith, and a genuine regard and enjoyment of one another. All of which means that when it came time to discuss what was happening in the Communion, there was a network of established relationships and mutual affection to build upon.

Some will no doubt find the description I am giving of no use to the Communion. It is of course easy to gather around differences when those gathering have no real skin in the game. An official from one diocese once told AEHS essentially the same thing during a lunchtime address. "It's all well and good," it was said, "that you do this now. When you're in the real world, you'll find it's not so easy." I find this view, however, to be too quickly dismissive of our common life in AEHS. The people who gather in AEHS take their churches and traditions seriously. Moreover, by the time Anglican students arrive at Duke, they have generally pursued a discernment process that has left them with real and vital ties to their own traditions—both institutionally and relationally. I admired my bishops and the stand they had taken for the faith once delivered to the saints. Others, who disagreed with us, admired their church's willingness to go out on the ledge for inclusivity. We were and are *invested* in the divisions of our Communion. And those divisions made themselves felt in various ways.

My wife and I lived with an Episcopal student and his wife in the same house. In many ways this was no great challenge; as Episcopalians go, Stephen was more like me than most. Indeed, I often found myself feeling like a liberal in conversations with him!

A House Divided?

It is not a stretch for me to say that they were our best friends at Duke. And yet we all became increasingly aware of the way the wounds in the Communion left their own mark in our friendship. There was always, simmering below the surface of things, the reality that my church exists because many people became convinced that his church was apostate. There was a suspicion that had to be guarded against, confessed, repented of, and forgiven. And with all that, it did not go away. The division itself calls into question things we hold to as matters of ultimate concern. This is true, not because of how anyone behaves but simply as a fact. Stephen is a good friend, a gracious interlocutor, and a holy man. And yet in many ways he exacerbates the problem for me. His presence in The Episcopal Church presses my judgments and discernments about things that matter more to me than anything else. And because we lived together and saw one another so regularly, the question was ongoing and persistent, there in the midst of things even when we were engaged in the mundane stuff of life. As we reflected upon our life together, Stephen and I became convinced over time that Church division is pervasive and generative, at least apparently so. The mere fact of it calls us into question in such a way that suspicion is almost inevitable. That suspicion creates an eagerness to be offended, making us prone to misunderstanding and producing even more to divide over.

And if this happens in the best of circumstances, one can only imagine the escalation that is possible when there are not so many sympathies from the start. What about when there are personal hurts along with real differences and principled objections? If in the best of circumstances our divisions create these issues, what about when no such circumstances obtain? When there are actual differences at play, what will be the fruit of suspicion, offense, and misunderstanding? What I have discovered in all of this is that what the Prayer Book calls our "unhappy divisions"[2] are unhappy precisely because they cripple our ability to discern the Spirit's movements in those we have already written off. Divisions have hermeneutic significance; they quite literally make us stupid. In

---

2. Episcopal Church, *Book of Common Prayer*, 818.

such a context, do we have any reason for confidence that we will go on "into all truth"?

The debates of our time may in the end be intractable. But it is certain that we will have no way of knowing this until we have put away caricature, invective, and ignorance of one another. And it is only in a context of ongoing refusal of these cheap weapons that the Spirit-enabled words of our speakers will have their intended effect. The intended contribution of AEHS to the life of the Communion is not that we believe we can solve debates that have taken the better part of a century to emerge; that would be naive indeed. Nor are the addresses to our House by the speakers contained here themselves our contribution. If we have something to offer to the Communion, it is a form of life that creates preconditions into which the voice of the Spirit might speak to prepared hearts. We contribute a life of common prayer and reception of the Scriptures, of regular fellowship with those whose opinions on the issues of the day differ widely from our own, of time spent "offline," learning what else there is in the world that matters to one another. And in this way, we have come truly to value one another's presence in our lives, to love one another as friends, sisters, and brothers. I am still myself deeply frustrated with the decisions of The Episcopal Church. But I am no longer able to caricature those decisions as merely the work of evil-minded people with no concern for the gospel or its truth. Such people there may be in the Episcopal ranks (and in my own too, for that matter). But I also know that within the camps of those who disagree strongly with me are decent, intelligent people who are eager to hear a word from God in a confusing time.

We believe that the way of life found in AEHS is not the least bit naïve; rather, we think, it is an utterly realistic way of dealing with the fact that none of us knows as fully as we ought. Meanwhile, the current circumstances in which the Church finds itself are pitched to deprive us of precisely those whom we need if we are to know the Lord more fully. I say "realistic" because we have no delusions about the entrenched nature of the issues that divide us. It has been the greater part of a decade since the formation of

A House Divided?

ACNA, and many other Anglican churches have been in existence for far longer. But we in AEHS believe that we have embraced a way of life that can be pursued in the Communion far in advance of a resolution to those issues (and I, for one, think it unlikely those issues will ever reach resolution apart from some such course of action as is recommended here).

First, we invite members and pastors of Episcopal and other Anglican congregations to begin to pray together as early and as often as may be. In the vision of Jo Bailey Wells, everything begins with common prayer. We invite them to say the Daily Office together; to hear the lectionary readings read out loud to both sides, and to respond with the Canticle acclamations. May each side hear the other's affirmation of thanks to God for the divine Word that addresses the Church. Virtually no agreement on what is meant by the Word is required in order to gather together, to hear the Word spoken, and to thank God for it. In the prayers, each can hear the other imploring that God's kingdom come and will be done, as in heaven so on earth. Again, there is virtually no agreement presupposed as to what that might mean. As in most of our traditions, the doing precedes (and we hope makes possible) the understanding. At AEHS it has been quite common to hear people praying for bishops who were (at the moment in which we prayed for them) opposing parties in a lawsuit. This was not comfortable, but it was possible and needful and helpful.

We invite severed members of Episcopal and other Anglican congregations and their pastors to experiments in informal gathering. Perhaps those gatherings could be recreational (congregations might join one another to participate in local marathons) or service related (volunteering together in soup kitchens or at Red Cross events). In either case, these members might actually get to know and appreciate one another for what is held in common (whatever that might be). Again, no agreement about what such events might be is presupposed; it may be that congregations find precious little that they can enjoy in common. What is presupposed is a willingness to do so if and when they discover it.

William Glass—*Afterword*

We suspect that common prayer and gatherings might go on for some time. At AEHS we were expected to commit for the duration of our time at Duke. Obviously commitments in less-structured environments would be negotiated in different ways, but on this as on most things, clergy may and must lead from the front. Over time, members of the divided Church will find themselves, we suspect, unable to persist in caricature of those with whom they disagree. At that point, when one party to a discussion feels it will not be misrepresented by the other, the kind of trust that allows a fierce conversation may emerge. And those conversations, while they may produce nothing more than an accurate and charitable understanding of just why one church feels it cannot yet fully commune with another, would themselves be an incredible improvement over what is visible in the current Anglican scene. If those who disagree can learn to treat one another with charity, that itself will be a work of God to be received with gratitude and hope.

AEHS takes as one of its constituent principles the challenge to "live with walls down." I was always ambivalent about that phrase. To the degree that "walls" are the unconscious aggressions we cherish towards one another, allowing our misunderstandings to go unchecked and our suspicions unexamined, I wholeheartedly endorse it. But there is a real sense in which some of these walls were built before us, by those with more authority than we have. We have inherited cities with walls raised for us and before us. These will take more work to level than we are yet able to do. It is worth saying that at the conclusion of my time at Duke, I was still unable in good conscience to receive Eucharist with many of my Episcopal brothers and sisters. And it must be said that there were some with whom I was never able to get beyond the minimal sharing of a common prayer service. In some cases, the wounds were deeper than could be reasonably healed in such a short time. It would be foolish not to reckon with that possibility in the Communion as well. But there are still days ahead in which that trust may yet be forged and another section of wall be dismantled. I mourn the existence (and, at least in my case, the necessity) of that wall, as I know many of my Episcopal friends do. But AEHS gave us a place to pound on it, to beat on it with all our might, so that those on the other side would know to what extent we mourned these unhappy divisions. AEHS forms ministers for the Anglican Communion by teaching them that the Church, to be the Church, must carry within its life the marks of the Lord's broken body. We affirm that it is in Christ's body that "the dividing wall" has been crushed (Eph 2:14). But even as we profess what has already been accomplished, we groan under the weight of all the ways that finished work is not yet apparent among us. And we invite the Church to experiment with us in displays of fierce charity, to stand at the wall in a vigil until the Lord sees fit to bring it down.

There is no brilliance in anything suggested here; the brilliance is to believe it is possible. If a wall must separate us for the time being, let the wall be also the means of our communication. Let us gather and listen, not so that we can abandon our convictions but so that we may understand them better. Whatever happens as a result of these experiments, we can be assured of God's favor upon them, for they represent nothing other than the attempt to speak the truth in love and to accept neither one without the vital other. We may be constrained at the end of the day (as I was) to worship without one another and to treat one another as a pagan or a tax collector (Matt 18:17). But it should be noted that we know how Jesus intended such people to be treated precisely because he was so often in their company. That may be the best we can do at the moment. Let us do it with all our might, as unto the Lord, for in doing so we may host angels unawares.

Bibliography

Allison, C. FitzSimons. *The Cruelty of Heresy: An Affirmation of Christian Orthodoxy*. New York: Morehouse, 1994.
Anglican Church in America. "The Affirmation of St. Louis (1977)." Accessed June 20, 2014. http://www.acahome.org/anglican_documents/anglican_documents_affirmation_of_st_louis.html.
Anglican Church in North America. "Our Genesis." Last modified February 8, 2013. http://www.anglicanchurch.net/media/Our_Genesis_revised_2.8_.13_.pdf.
Anglican Communion Covenant Design Group. "An Anglican Covenant—The Third (Ridley Cambridge) Draft." Accessed June 20, 2014. http://www.anglicancommunion.org/media/100850/ridley_cambridge_covenant_english.pdf.
Anglican Episcopal House of Studies. "Frequently Asked Questions." Accessed June 26, 2014. http://divinity.duke.edu/initiatives-centers/aehs/what-students-need-know.
Anglicans for Comprehensive Unity. "Status of Covenant Adoption." Last updated January 27, 2015. http://noanglicancovenant.org/background.htm#status.
Avis, Paul D. L. *Anglicanism and the Christian Church: Theological Resources in Historical Perspective*. New York: T. & T. Clark, 2002.
Badertscher, Eric A. "The Measure of a Bishop: The *Episcopari Vagantes*, Apostolic Succession, and the Legitimacy of the Anglican 'Continuing Church' Movement." MA thesis, Gordon Conwell Theological Seminary, 1998. http://anglicanhistory.org/essays/badertscher/index.html.
Bergen, Doris L. *Twisted Cross: The German Christian Movement in the Third Reich*. Chapel Hill: University of North Carolina Press, 1996.
Cassidy, Joseph P. "Radical Anglicanism: A Vision for the Future." In *The Hope of Things to Come: Anglicanism and the Future*, edited by Mark D. Chapman, 88–101. New York: Mowbray, 2010.
Cheshire, Joseph Blount. *The Church in the Confederate States: A History of the Protestant Episcopal Church in the Confederate States*. New York: Longmans, Green, 1912.

Bibliography

Consultation of Anglican Bishops in Dialogue. "A Testimony of Our Journey toward Reconciliation." Statement prepared by the Fifth Consultation of Anglican Bishops in Dialogue, Coventry, England, May 2014.

Episcopal Church. *The Book of Common Prayer*. New York: Church Publishing, 1979.

———. *Constitution and Canons of the Episcopal Church*. New York: Episcopal Church Center, 2012.

Episcopal News Service. "Deputies Protest Robinson Confirmation." News release, August 6, 2003. http://www.episcopalarchives.org/cgi-bin/ENS/ENSpress_release.pl?pr_number=2003-235-A.

———. "New Hampshire Priest Is First Openly Gay Man Elected Bishop." News release, June 7, 2003. http://archive.episcopalchurch.org/3577_18284_ENG_HTM.htm.

Faith and Order Commission. "The Unity of the Church: Gift and Calling; The Canberra Statement." World Council of Churches. Last modified February 20, 1991. http://www.oikoumene.org/en/resources/documents/wcc-commissions/faith-and-order-commission/i-unity-the-church-and-its-mission/the-unity-of-the-church-gift-and-calling-the-canberra-statement.

General Convention of The Episcopal Church. *Journal of the General Convention of The Episcopal Church, Columbus, 2006*. New York: Episcopal Church Center, 2006.

———. *Journal of the General Convention of The Episcopal Church, Denver, 2000*. New York: Episcopal Church Center, 2000.

———. *Journal of the General Convention of The Episcopal Church, Detroit, 1988*. New York: Episcopal Church Center, 1988.

———. *Journal of the General Convention of The Episcopal Church, Indianapolis, 1994*. New York: Episcopal Church Center, 1994.

———. *Journal of the General Convention of The Episcopal Church, Indianapolis, 2012*. New York: Episcopal Church Center, 2012.

———. *Journal of the General Convention of the Episcopal Church*, Minneapolis, 2003. New York: Episcopal Church Center, 2003.

———. *Journal of the General Convention of The Episcopal Church*, Philadelphia, 1997. New York: Episcopal Church Center, 1997.

———. *Journal of the General Convention of The Episcopal Church*, Phoenix, 1991. New York: Episcopal Church Center, 1991.

Global Anglican Future Conference. "The Jerusalem Declaration." Global Anglican Future Conference. Published August 4, 2013. http://gafcon.org/the-jerusalem-declaration.

Global Fellowship of Confessing Anglicans. "What You Need to Know about GAFCON and the GFCA." Accessed June 2, 2014. http://fca.net/about.

Griswold, Frank T. "The Presiding Bishop Writes to the Bishops before General Convention." Office of the Presiding Bishop of The Episcopal Church. Published June 13, 2003. http://www.episcopalchurch.org/library/article/presiding-bishop-writes-bishops-general-convention.

Bibliography

Guelzo, Allen C. *For the Union of Evangelical Christendom: The Irony of the Reformed Episcopalians*. University Park: Pennsylvania State University Press, 1994.

Kasper, Walter. *Harvesting the Fruits: Basic Aspects of Christian Faith in Ecumenical Dialogue*. New York: Continuum, 2009.

Lash, Nicholas. *Theology for Pilgrims*. London: Darton, Longman & Todd, 2008.

Mason, Arthur J. *The Church of England and the Episcopacy*. Cambridge: Cambridge University Press, 1888.

Miller, Samuel. *Letters concerning the Constitution and Order of the Christian Ministry Addressed to the Members of the Presbyterian Churches in the City of New York: To Which Is Prefixed a Letter on the Present Aspect & Bearing of the Episcopal Controversy by Samuel Miller*. New York: Hogan, 1830.

Office of Communication of The Episcopal Church. *A Response to the Invitation of the Windsor Report ¶135*. New York: Episcopal Church Center, 2005.

Prichard, Robert W. *A History of the Episcopal Church*. Harrisburg: Morehouse, 1991.

Radner, Ephraim. *A Brutal Unity: The Spiritual Politics of the Christian Church*. Waco: Baylor University Press, 2012.

Reformed Episcopal Church. "The Reformed Episcopal Church: A Brief History." Accessed June 20, 2014. http://rechurch.org/history.html.

Traycik, Louis C. "The Continuing Church: Past, Present, and Future—Two Views." *The Christian Challenge* (website). Last modified September 30, 2009. http://www.challengeonline.org/modules/news/article.php?storyid=236. Site discontinued.

Vatican Council II. "Unitatis Redintegratio: Decree on Ecumenism." Accessed June 2, 2014. http://www.vatican.va/archive/hist_councils/ii_vatican_council/documents/vat-ii_decree_19641121_unitatis-redintegratio_en.html.

Weil, Simone. *La Pesanteur et la Grâce*. Paris: Librarie Plon, 1947.

Wesley, Charles. *The Manuscript Journal of The Reverend Charles Wesley*, M.A. 2 vols. Eds. S. T. Kimbrough, Jr., and Kenneth G.C. Newport. Nashville: Abingdon, 2008.

Williams, Rowan. "Trinity and Revelation." *Modern Theology* 2.3 (1986) 197–212.

www.ingramcontent.com/pod-product-compliance
Lightning Source LLC
Chambersburg PA
CBHW050837160426
43192CB00011B/2056